I LOVE BEING OLD

The last phase of life can be made the best

Armiger L Jagoe

ISBN: 1545445095
ISBN 13: 9781545445099

TABLE OF CONTENTS

KICK OFF

Day after day we wait
not knowing
the depth
our well.

Sara Schneidman

I wish I could have talked with Gill Pharaoh, before she planned to have herself killed.

"Gill," I would have said, "I think what you intend to do is as strange as seeing a runner, who, on a crisp fall day, nears the finish line where there are rewards with red flags waving and a joyful celebration awaiting him, and he suddenly walks off the track.

"The fourth and last stage of existence can be made the best. Revel in the sweetness of life. You have a unique capacity to continue engaging with your existence and loving fully. Life is not an exercise to be endured; it is a mystery to be enjoyed. Give up your passive decision for living. My friend, don't drop your ice cream cone."

Gill was a London nurse, 75-years-old and in good health. She decided to go to the Lifecircle Clinic in Basel, Switzerland, to have a fatal injection that ended her life.

In a blog publication, she wrote, "I am not whinging. Neither am I depressed. Day by day I am enjoying my life. I simply do not want to follow this natural deterioration through the last stage when I may require a lot of help."

I love being old and don't want to be a day younger. I like to cram each twenty-four hours with awareness, discovery, appreciation and fun. I delight in proving that enjoying your final stage of life can be made great. There is no one else I had rather be.

Glad to have graduated from the octogenarian table, these are my thoughts for each day:

Today is my birthday.
I want to make everywhere I go a place of springs.
I am going to laugh a lot and sing a song.
I am going to experience a miracle.
It's refreshing to learn something new.
I will be alert to notice the special color for the day.
I hope to achieve many accomplishments—large and small.
It's exciting to know that tomorrow is going to be even more
    enjoyable than today. And a bad day lasts only 24 hours.
I dare to dream.
I realize that God is in love with me, and vice versa.

I'll show you how I do it.

One of the flaws in the English language is not having a pronoun to refer to both sexes. For example, "hes" could give a choice of either "he" or "she". As I don't have time for the grammar experts to accept my recommendation, throughout the book when I use "he", consider it as "hes".

MY PURPOSE IN WRITING

Life is lived forward,
but understood backward.

Soren Kierkegaad

I was stunned by the title of an article by Dr. Ezekiel Emanuel. It was "Why I Hope to Die at 75". My achieving age 75 was followed by two joyful decades of newness, excitement and fun. It rivaled the earlier stages of my life in being the best.

We tend to think about aging as matter of bodies wearing out, as automobiles do. But the analogy is not a good one. And automobile original parts will indeed wear out but an adult human is not operation with his original parts. We are made of cells that are continually taking in nutrients and dividing, replacing old parts with new ones. I admire the octopus that has no tendency to decline with old age. It just keeps going and reproducing until some accident or predator get hold of it.

I now have time to look into the depths of my personal evolution and enjoy being perspective with a richer way of thinking about my life. It is an attempt to unravel and trace back all the tangled threads of my being - an unfolding and dynamic journey in thought that follows the thematic designs through my life.

While lulling in delightful old age, I feel obligated to record things about my life which future relatives might find of interest. I get encouraging advice from what a Psalmist writer wrote 1,800 years ago.

> "I will utter hidden things, things from of old – things we have heard and known, things our ancestors have told us, so the next generation will know them, even the children yet to be born."

Years ago when I conducted workshops for writing memoirs, I would ask how many wish they knew more about their grandparents. Every hand went up. I don't want my future ken to raise their hand when asked this question.

Charley Kempthorne sets a good example. At age 78, he wakes before sunrise and after a cup of black coffee writes in his journal, about his past and other reflections. He said that "most of my journal has been and continues to be an end in itself. It helps me understand my life better. Or maybe it just makes me feel better and get started on the day in a better mood."

In writing about my life, I see myself anew with a fresh vision of me and my purpose. It is an awakening to a world of seemingly endless riches.

And, perhaps, recording this is my means of suggestion.

OUR STAGES OF LIFE

There is no cure for birth or death
save to enjoy the in-between.

George Santayana

I love being old because I have time to relate my stages of life
to the seasons of the year. It makes close the distant past. For
example, the earth time of spring can be compared to our initial
green Awareness Stage, which begins at birth, lush with discovery.

Even though I cannot recall life before two or three-years-of-
age, I can imagine the sensation, after nine months of being com-
fortably enclosed with rudimentary consciousness inside a warm
body to suddenly being exposed to light, sound, and the feeling of
being held by a big human being. With this shocking experience,
a baby's response when its lungs first fill with air is to cry.

I was born at home in Okolona, Mississippi, and my grandmother was in the room when this event occurred. As she was po-
litically minded, I suspect the first sound I heard was her saying, "I
hope he'll be a Democrat."

The green Awareness Stage is a sponge for absorbing newness, similar to Nature sprouting fresh green leaves. With the awakening of senses, a baby experiences colors, sounds, odors, hunger and touch. Tests confirm an infant benefits by being touched, held, cuddled and sung to. The famed architect, Frank Lloyd Wright, claimed that his career was sparked by his mother hanging in the nursery pictures of famed cathedrals.

While in a shopping center, I am fascinated at the direct eye-contact I get from an infant being carried by parents. Humor is important at this initial stage of life and nothing is more contagious than a baby's chuckle.

With the first unaided step, a child begins the yellow Achieving Stage, which is the second and longest period of life, like an endless summer. The act of being able to toddle across a room is a major accomplishment. This is followed by decades of advancing both physically and mentally, with new experiences, new insights and possibilities. Achieving and competing against both others and self is ingrained in this long stage.

As a clue to the third period of life, what does one do after riding a bike up a steep incline and seeing ahead a long downhill stretch of road? He coasts. Providing one is satisfied in relaxing from his yellow Achieving Stage, this time can be enjoyable.

The third and blue Coasting period is like the refreshing fall months, lush with bright autumn colors. It is time to take stock of what has been accomplished and to enjoy relaxation. This is when I did many of the things on my bucket list of things to do. I made sure I wasn't riding a dead horse. I also dedicated time to leisure and cultivating the seeds of virtue.

While physically able, during my blue Coasting stage, I did a lot of traveling. St. Augustine wrote that the world is a book and those who do not travel read only a page. During this third period, I visited every place I had wanted to see.

This ranged from Machu Pichia to Angkor Wat. I visited the jungle temples and the boat people in Cambodia, and enjoyed a

Buddhist retreat in Japan. I went zip-lining in New England and hang gliding in New Zealand. None of these I could do today. But I have done it.

As the fourth and climax winter season of life, the purple Giving Back Stage can be made the best. It should be exhilarating, and it's a crime to let it pass without being enjoyed to the hilt. Albert Camus said, "In the depth of winter, I finally learned that within me there lay an invincible summer."

This is prime time for fresh growth and nourishing the seed of self-knowledge. In winter, leaf-barren trees enable one to see through the woods. I now enjoy viewing through my woods I have cultivated for decades. There I discover many interesting things about myself.

When enjoying my purple Giving Back Stage, others and I benefit by my generosity of self and of my possessions. In down-sizing, if I own something I cannot give away, I don't possess it, it possesses me.

To maximize the delight of being old, it is necessary to incorporate into each day the first three stages of life. Enjoy acts of green Awareness and yellow Achieving. And daily naps can account for blue Coasting.

The excitement of today can be fueled by appreciation of the past and anticipation of a fun tomorrow. I stick my hand in the fire and shout. "I love being old!"

TMBOOE

(tim-boo'e)
Blessed are those who know they are blessed.

An unrecorded beatitude

My imagined organization, Tmbooe, Ltd., would have its creed the poem, *Invocation to Usha*, written by Kalidasa in the 4th century:

> Look to this day
> for it is Life.
> Yesterday is but a dream,
> and tomorrow is only
> a vision, but
> today, well spent
> makes every yesterday
> a dream of happiness, and
> every tomorrow
> a vision of hope.

For friends I posed this situation. "If an organization, known as TMBOOE, Ltd, were conducting a search to discover the most blessed one on earth, would you submit your name?" Here are some of the responses:

Successful author: "Why not? What would I have to lose?"
Housewife: "I'm not sure, because it is all relative."
Man in advertising world: "I like that concept. I think it might sell."
Banker: "I suspect there is a cost involved."
Woman executive: "No, because I assume it would automatically give my name to 100 organizations which would start flooding my e-mail."
Bulgarian food server: "No, because I'm not blessed."

Others whom I have quizzed are too handicapped from inner paralysis to give serious thought. I find this discouraging because counting one's blessings is a means of saying ecstatically "Thanks!" to a Superior Being who keeps a compassionate eye on all. I think it inconsiderate to let a blessing slip unappreciated. I don't want to feel adrift in uncharted waters.

As happiness doesn't come from outside, I encourage everyone to submit his name to TMBOOE. I would, and if I won, I would put the designation TMBOOE after my name. And if I were not declared the winner, I would demand a re-count.

BAGGAGE

He manages like somebody carrying a box
that is too heavy.
And ends with "he can go on without ever
putting the box down."

From "Michiko Dead" poem
Jack Gilbert

The past is never past, and I try to remember only that which gives pleasure. I love being old because I have time to be sure I am traveling light. I don't allow time for brooding over dislikes, grudges and the many mistakes I have made. I realize you can't unscramble an egg, and I take a lesson from the weather because it pays no attention to criticism.

The singer and poet, Leonard Cohen, said a pessimist is someone who is waiting for it to rain. He complains about reality's complexities and gloats on the bad or sad things in life. I remember a woman who lived her life on a minor key, moaning about vanished joys.

She dampened my cheerful 'Hello' by saying, "It has been six months and eight days since my husband died, and I miss him so much." Her twisted face looked as if she had just driving home from the funeral.

I was tempted to say:

What about the good times you had together?
Think of something you shared with him that was fun.
What did you two do to please the other?
Don't cry because it's over; smile because it happened.
Remember the vacations you enjoyed together.
Aren't you lucky he didn't dump you for a mistress?
But I didn't, and I left her wallowing in her misery.

Tchaikovsky was also one who loaded himself down with negative thinking. When he was 32-years-old, he wrote to his brother, "How can I be happy, knowing that every day I am one day closer to my grave?"

Another cheerful soul, whom I would not have invited for coffee at Starbucks, was Thomas Hobbes. In 1651 said, "Life is solitary, poor, nasty, brutish and short." With this attitude, I bet he could have counted his friends with the fingers of one hand.

My thinking ill of the few who have taken advantage of me has no effect on them, but it can tear me up. By assuring this doesn't happen, I pray for them. I don't want to be like the old codger in the church meeting.

At the end of his sermon on "Forgiveness", the minister asked those who had no enemies or people they disliked to come forward. There followed a long period of embarrassing silence. Finally, an old man with the aid of two canes slowly made his way down the aisle to the front of the church.

Beaming with joy, the minister shouted, "Hallelujah! Congratulations and blessings upon you, brother. Now, tell us how you have accomplished the Christian achievement of having no enemies?"

He said, "I outlived them bastards."

I find that forgiving must be accompanied by forgetting. For many years after her retirement, each month I would take Mabel to lunch. She had been my secretary when I started my business. Now, she was quite old and living in a retirement community.

One day after we were seated at our table, she said, "I want you to know I have forgiven you and forgotten the time you threw a pencil at me."

With wide eyes, I asked her what she was talking about.

"One day when you were leaving the office, you stopped at my desk, made a note, then threw the pencil at me and left."

I had no idea what she was talking about. Then she said, "But don't give it a second thought because I have forgiven you and completely wiped it out of my mind."

When we had finished lunch and were waiting for the check, I said, "Mabel, about the pencil incident, perhaps it was one of those hectic Monday mornings when I might have been rushed to get to a meeting."

"No," she said, "it was Wednesday."

VOICES FROM THE PAST

We hear only our own voices, still echoes,
returning to our emptiness.

Dejan Stojanovic

A voice is as distinctive as a photograph. Last week I received a call and heard a woman say, "Hello, Jay."

I immediately responded, "Barbara, it is good to hear from you." The person calling was the delightful English widow of a college classmate and someone I hadn't heard from in over a year. On the wings of memory when I heard her voice, it was as if she were standing in front of me.

I love being old because, from the deep echoes of my past, I have time to tune in on certain voices. Like passing shadows, they are like a beam of light into the closet of my brain. I enjoy recalling the unique tone of voice and words spoken by those who have been special during my life – many are my TMBOOE sources. For example, one of the early voices from my youth was that of Laura, our cook and my nurse.

She was a very large and positive African-American. Although I wasn't there when she said it, many times I have heard my father's account of the spring morning when the chickens were sounding in the backyard and he walked into the kitchen of our house in northern Mississippi to tell Laura the family was moving down to the Gulf Coast.

Father said she took off her stripped apron and asked in her husky voice, referring to me "Is you taking the baby with you? " When father nodded with a smile, Laura said, "I'm going, too."

As my protector and later close friend, Laura was stingy with her words. When stung in a leg by a stingray, which normally required hospitalization, she refused medical help. Moaning in agony, she kept saying, "Pain—it got purpose."

Mrs. Airey, my white-haired first grade teacher had the soothing voice of a concerned grandmother. I was quite tongue-tied, and this sweet soul would whisper, "Armiger, now say that again… slowly."

Our cook, little Eunice, who for twelve years became like a beloved family member, had a light and happy voice. One evening when mother came home, Eunice told her, "Mrs. Gardiner called and said when you come to the D. A. R. luncheon tomorrow to bring along a copy of Mr. Lincoln's jitterbug dress."

The only time I remember hearing Eunice being excited was when she shot Buddy in the head. He was our giant-sized gardener and her boy-friend, whom she discovered had been "messing around with a woman from Turkey Creek".

"Lord God!" Eunice cried, "I didn't mean to kill him—I just wanted to wing him!"

This incident had a pleasant ending. It turned out that Eunice had a weak pistol and the bullet from the back of Buddy's neck was easily removed in the hospital. I was surprised at what a good shot she was. She spent only an hour in jail, and next week, Buddy, who had gotten the message, was back again working in the yard.

Tom Anderson, owner of Anderson's Men's Wear where I worked when in high school, was the kindest man in town. I never saw him, not in a suit and wearing a stiff collar. "Mr. Tom" spoke with a slight hesitation as if he was afraid of offending someone. During the four years I worked in the store, with his sought advice, he became like my surrogate father. Today, I can still hear his voice.

One Saturday evening, after work we were having a sandwich at the nearby drug store, and I asked him what I should do. I had invited two girls to the same dance. Mr. Tom listened carefully, then said, "Armitage (he never could get my name straight), I think ---- perhaps----- well, it might be a good idea----maybe---- if you got sick."

Mrs. Estelle Heiss, who was the self-appointed historian in town, spoke with authority, "Now you listen to what I am going to tell you, and you pay attention. This is valuable information. Don't treat it lightly. You hear what I am going to tell you, and don't you ever forget it."

Cindy Crump, who was a collector of gossip, would say in a whiney voice, "Now, I don't want to gossip---it might not be true----but I thought you should know----perhaps is really might not have happened---but it could have-----so I think I have the right to tell you ……"

Mrs. Rodger was our neighbor who flattered me by saying, at night, she enjoyed lying in bed and listening to me practicing my squeaking clarinet. I thought her cheerful voice sounded like little bells ringing.

Our other neighbor was Mrs. Matthews, who had a cheerful and shy voice. Back then the Pet Milk people came out with canned milk. They offered a reward to those who sent in the best limericks about their new product. One day, Mrs. Matthews, who had not sent an entry, was surprised to receive a $50 check from Pet Milk. The accompanying letter said that although she would appreciate why they couldn't publish her limerick, they felt it deserved their gift.

Later, Dickie, her twelve-year-old son, confessed he had sent an entry under his mother's name. Attempting to be embarrassed, Mrs. Matthews smiled when she read it to us.

No teats to pull,
no manure to pitch,
just punch a hole
in the son of a bitch.

Myrtie Hutchens, a teacher who boarded with us, had a high and monotone voice with no flicks of humor. One night during dinner, she said, "You have to be careful how you correct your pupil's English. This morning, little Tommy Edwards was excited, telling the other students, 'Last night, Mummy went to the hospital and Daddy and me slept together.'"

Myrtie said, "I told him, 'No, Tommy, last night Daddy and **I** slept together. His face lighted up and he said, 'Did you, Miss Hutchens? You must have come in when I was asleep.'"

My father was a quiet man, and I can't recall ever hearing him raise his voice. He said much with a nod or shake of his head.

Mother was a grown-up Southern belle, who thought she was boring unless she was talking. When she heard something disturbing, she would say, "Lord, have mercy, have mercy."

With her pleasant but firm voice she let you know how she thought the dance should be danced. I can still hear the advice she gave Nelson Eddy, when as a young baritone was beginning his successful career.

During the years of a concert series Mother organized to be performed in the high school auditorium, we would have the singer or musician for dinner the night before his performance. The evening that Nelson Eddy was our guest, she told him, "Now, Son, you want to be sure your singing is appreciated. Keep in mind that you are preforming for a Southern audience."

With a nod, he smiled and said, "Mrs. Jagoe, I assure you I have thought about that. And in my repertoire I am including *Mama's little baby loves shortnin', shortnin'. Mama's little baby loves shortnin' bread*."

A family friend, Minnie McGill, not only monopolized conversation but took an option on the next one. She would stop speaking and say, "When I finish tell you this, remind me to tell you about something else."

J. K. Vardaman was my father's age and was one of my closest friends. He had a husky dry voice and chose his words carefully. We enjoyed kidding one another. One day I called him and said, "Today is Father's Day and I especially wanted to talk with you."

I could sense he was tightening up.

"So?" he said.

"On Father's Day I have a special something to say to you."

Silence on the other end of the phone.

Then I said, "I am calling just to let you know how grateful I am that you are not my father."

There was a barking laugh, and I heard him shout to his wife, "Bea, come talk with this idiot. I picked up the phone by mistake."

WOW!

In Okinawa where people are noted for their longevity, they have a notion of *ikigai,* which is their reason for getting out of bed in the morning. It is a means of clothing one's self with joy.

Ikigai requires a deep self-search for the foundation of a reason to enjoy life and to give maximum value to one's existence. It is motivation to live life to the fullest. This I need as a springboard into each new and exciting day of a world made new.

Like the Anhinga bird which has to dry its wet wings before it can fly, when I wake up, I make it a practice to say ten "WOW's" before I get to the bathroom. I have many sources of wonderness for a WOW!

- I can see with my right eye – my left eye – and they coordinate sight!
- I can touch my fingers together!

- I can get out of bed on my own!
- By cautiously putting one foot in front of the other, I can walk!
- I hear the tingling of a clock!
- I can feel the floor with my bare feet!
- When I turn on the switch, light turns on!
- I remember where the bathroom is!
- When I twist the faucet, water will flow!
- The water is both hot and cold!
- We on earth are spinning through space at 1,000 miles an hour!
- It's great that I am not one of the wealthy who have become janitors of their possessions!
- The World Health Organization said today the average male age is 69 years, and I'm 95!

I remember what St. Paul told the Corinthians, "Our inner self is being renewed day by day." And I get excited and marvel at the wonder of my being. Hope has been called the forgotten virtue of our time, so I put hope in action and try to make it a regular practice. I feel like a kid on Christmas morning.

I have found that what might become boring moments can be made enjoyable. When I am the captive audience for a dull person, I have learned how to become a winner. I think "Wow" and put on my Duchenne smile, which I do by grinning, then flexing the muscles at the sides of my mouth.

I think it important every day to have both many Wows, and to say a multitude of "thanks". Elie Wiesel said, "When a person doesn't have gratitude, something is missing in his or her humanity. A person can almost be defined by his or her attitude toward gratitude."

I reconsider my TMBOOE application and think "Wow!"

CAN YOU FIND AN
ORDINARY PERSON?

*The ordinary takes on a glow
and wonder all of its own.*

Mike A. Lancaster

In enjoying old age, I know the answer to the possibility of finding an ordinary person is "no way."

Of the over seven billion people on our planet, no two have the same fingerprint. Among this mass of humanity you won't an exact duplicate in physique, mental capacity, experience and personality. It's exciting to realize that everyone is special, and that someone is out there is eager to be discovered.

Sociologists at Duke University published a study on isolation in America. They found that over the past two decades Americans' circle of close friend has shrunk dramatically. Twice as many people reported they had no one with whom they can share important matters. To our detriment, we have become a country of individuals with too many strangers.

When I grew up in Gulfport, Mississippi, our house on the beach was a mile from downtown. We knew the name of everyone living along this stretch. Walking along the street it was unusual to see someone you didn't know. But today, things have changed. I don't know four of the nine people who live in my condo floor, and I sense that they do not want to be known.

One time I did the unpardonable thing of speaking to a stranger in an English tea room. While sitting with my wife, I noticed three very dignified women sitting at the end of the room. Two were very busy with animated talk and the third—dressed in purple—seemed bored.

As they passed in leaving, I touched the third woman and said, "Thank you for wearing my favorite color." She ignored me as if she had accidently brushed against a column. Ten minutes later she returned.

"Pardon me," she said hesitantly, in the Queen's English, "I am afraid you mistook me for someone you know."

I said, "No, I wanted to compliment you on how delightful you look in wearing my favorite color."

She stood motionless and gave this thought. Then she began to melt and said, "My husband also likes to see me wear purple." She added, "Did you notice my necklace, which I made?"

My wife and I admired her necklace and asked how she had become a jewelry designer. After she had stood talking for five minutes, with open ears we asked her to sit with us. Although she learned nothing about us, we found out that she had gone to school in France, her husband was a retired banker, she had two children and one adorable granddaughter and she did volunteer work in an art gallery. We had become such close friends we thought she was going to stay for dinner.

I open a stranger by saying, "Tell me about you." I find I am like an oil miner who, every time he sticks his pick in the ground, strikes a gusher. It never fails. However, I don't try it on someone working for me on an hourly basis.

Often in crowded restaurant, airport terminal, packed bus or other place where there are a lot of people, I act like Peter Pan's Tinker Bell. I silently give a blessing for the each one there. It gives me a good feeling to act as a billionaire with a special gift for every person in sight. Who knows? ---it might be effective, and the price is right. And I get a tingle for having become aware of others.

If I were the President, I would give every citizen the obligation each day to befriend an ordinary person. Soon we would become an "us", rather than a "me" country. If this were achieved, within a year we would be a revitalized nation.

The world is filled with people, many within my reach, eager to become acknowledged as extraordinary persons. When I take advantage of this, my secret wealth increases in abundance.

HISTORY IN THE PALM OF MY HAND

We are not makers of history.
We are made by history.

Martin Luther King, Jr.

I love being old because although I can't relive my life, I am take delight in revisiting many important events I have experienced. Historical consciousness can be fun. Long-forgotten things live again and confirm my TMBOOE claim.

My first touch with fame came when I was eight and the circus was coming to town. Hoping to get a free ticket by offering to help, at dawn that morning I rode my bike out to the fairgrounds where they were putting up the big tent. A woman with bright red hair said, "Hey, kid, do you want to help me feed my horses?"

I jumped at the offer and worked to bring water for Glorious Gloria with her Famed Arabian Horses. When I finished, she gave me a ticket for the night show.

That evening I was sitting on a bleacher inside the tent when Glorious Gloria trotted by with her beautiful horses. I waved my arms and shouted like crazy. I was sure she saw me, and I was the proudest kid in town.

In 1932, my father had begun working in Washington, and he promised if Franklin Roosevelt were elected president, I could come up for the Inauguration. He was elected, and at age twelve I took the day-and-half Pullman train trip from Gulfport, Mississippi, to the Nation's Capital, where I first experienced frigid cold weather.

On March 4th, 1933, all I remember about the Inauguration in the East Portico was the mass of people, seeing the new President and the squawking loud speaker. During the following week while Father was working at his office in the Capitol Building, the place became my playground. The guards took me under their wing and told me some of the building's secrets.

In the echo rotunda, I could stand at one side and because of the dome ceiling I could hear conversation from someone at the far side of the room. The best secret was the hidden escape passageway that ran next to the wide main corridor. When Father and I were going to the other end of the building, I would take delight in sneaking into a special panel, then race down the passageway and be waiting for him when he got there.

That summer when I was thirteen and the Gulf was warm for swimming, the historic sailing ship *USS Constitution* known *Old Ironsides* was being towed for display around the country. It was coming to Gulfport. I knew that Paul Revere made both the spikes that held the hull together and the copper sheathing on the outside. It had helped to win the War of 1812. This I had to see.

Early that morning, I rowed in a light fog out into the Gulf to wait for its arrival. Like a whisper in the dark, suddenly this magnificent vessel loomed out of the mist right in front of me. The massive hull was like a moving sea mountain. A long towline from a tugboat pulled this tremendous ship through the water, and it seemed to be moving on its own. I heard the creaking noises of the waves against high white sides. I gave me goose pimples.

As it passed, with respect I stood up in my rowboat until it was out of sight.

In the winter of 1941, Churchill came to spend the Christmas holiday with President Roosevelt. I remember being with many others on the White House grounds, near a side balcony where Churchill came out to greet us. We were each bundled up with a bitter cold wind. Although we were not yet in the war, we had great empathy for the British people.

I remember Churchill using both arms to give us his victory sign. Then he shouted, "We shall win!" We cheered madly.

During my first year at Harvard, Wallace Stegner, my young professor who was teaching writing, invited me and another student to spend an evening with Robert Frost. We sat at the floor, listening as these two men talked. I still remember the conversation.

Robert Frost told about his recent visitor, who told him that he and his wife always enjoyed breakfast every morning in their small sunroom. He said since his wife died a month ago, every morning, a red cardinal had come and perched on a branch outside the window. He asked the poet if he thought this might be his wife's spirit.

Robert Frost said, "I told him 'Why not'."

In December, 1943, I had just gotten my wings in the Army Air Corps and was on home leave in Washington. Christmas afternoon, my mother and I stopped by the Wardman Park to see Aunt Mary, who was recovering from the flu. While visiting with her in her bedroom, the doorbell rang and I went to open it.

When I did, I went into shock. Standing there was grinning five-star General Eisenhower in his shirtsleeves. I froze. The General laughed, came in and shook my hand, "Glad to meet you, Lieutenant."

The Eisenhowers had the apartment upstairs, and Ike had snuck from England to spend Christmas with Mamie. Before we left after our visit, Ike's aide came in and asked us not to let anyone know for ten days that we had seen the General. He explained that the German's were anticipating the Allies' landing on the continent, and they would know it wouldn't happen while he was in America.

The only other time I saw Eisenhower was during the 1952 Republican Convention in Chicago when I was working with "Vets for Ike". Often he dropped in the room where we were working to give us thanks and encouragement.

I chuckle when I remember special things about long ago. When I was overseas, I received a letter from my mother, saying, "We had an unusual week. I was looking forward to a reception at the White House, but when we arrived there, we found we were a day late. I blamed this on your father who didn't want to go because he has a grudge against President Roosevelt. But the day wasn't wasted because we came home for me to change my hat and go to a cocktail party at the Mayflower Hotel."

In 1944, when we were flying bombing missions from Corsica, early one morning before take-off while we were at our plane on the hard-stand, suddenly the General drove up in his jeep with Doris Duke, then considered the wealthiest woman in America. She was in a Red Cross uniform, doing publicity work for the war effort.

She was a bit chunky with a face that had seen some wear. During a brief visit, she posed for the photographer while she faked shooting one of our turret guns. After they left, Mac McCullough, one of our gunners, said very softly, "She sure is beautiful—in a financial sort of way."

During the Truman administration, Margaret Truman was often part of the social group I enjoyed. She was a delightful and very unassuming girl, and a good dancer. It was then that President Truman wrote a blistering letter to a music critic who was critical of his daughter's singing.

I saw President Truman only one time. The year he was out of office I was having lunch in a restaurant when he walked in. Instinctively, I stood and applauded. Most of the other eaters did also. The ex-President beamed with a broad smile.

In 1953, as president of our Junior Chamber of Commerce, I was presiding over a dinner when Senator Joe McCarthy was our speaker. It wasn't an enjoyable experience. He didn't look clean, and he hadn't shaved for a few days. There was minimum conversation between the two of us, and instead of eating he had one brandy after the other.

When it came time for him to speak, he was a basket case. He had received national attention by his claim that the Soviets had invaded our State Department. During his talk that evening, as he shuffled papers in front of him, he kept shouting, "I can give you their names! They also have infiltrated Hollywood!"

Then, under his breath, he called to his secretary, who was sitting below, "Help, Jeannie. I need you!" She didn't budge.

On November 25, 1963, I drove my family down to Constitutional Avenue to witness the passing funeral procession of President Kennedy. Today, at age fifty, my older son recalls, "That was the first time I saw Dad cry."

One summer when we were in Spain, I took the family to a special Salvador Dali Happening in a nearby village. There I was in the front line of a crowd when the star come out from a building with his pointed black moustache and preceded by a row of chorus girls chanting, "Dali! Dali! Dali!"

When he passed by me, I held up my five-year-old daughter and said, "Please, paint my child." He stopped, laughed and smeared green paint on her forehead. Now, as a conversation gem, I can say, "Did you know that Dali painted my daughter?"

In 1974, I was chairman of a benefit at the Pan American Building for the International Eye Foundation. I was a prude and objected when I found that Elizabeth Taylor was to be the honorary chairman. I was critical of her many marriages.

At the beginning of the event, I was inside the building when I was told she had arrived and I had to go greet her. Elizabeth Taylor and her husband, Senator John Warner, were getting out of their limousine. She looked up at the 20 steps into the building and asked if there was an elevator. When the guard told her there was none, the Senator said, "Ok, Liz, we're going home."

He told me her back was out and it would be impossible for her to manage the steps. "No," she said, "I promised to come and I will."

Then she said to me, "If you take one arm and John takes the other, I think I can make it."

We slowly made our way with her silent anguish at every step. When we reached the top, through her tears, she gave a triumphant smile. I admired so much her courage that I leaned over and kissed her on the cheek and said, "You are indeed beautiful!"

My wife, who saw this, whispered in my ear, "You hypocrite."

Later I saw Senator Warner at a meeting when he told an amusing story. He was visiting a very rural part of the state when he stopped in a small general store and asked for a glass of water. The grumpy woman back of the counter said, "We only got sodas for sale."

Nearby her husband said, "Missy, that fellow he married to Elizabeth Taylor."

The Senator said she studied him, and then said, "You can have all the goddamed water you want."

The only time I have been in the White House was for a small reception in 1984. It was mid-summer, and I made the faux pas of wearing a bright bow tie, instead of a black one. My memento of this evening is a picture of President Reagan smiling at my tie and one of Nancy glaring at her husband, who was charmed by my wife.

Ah, age. Thanks for the TMBOOE memories.

ACHIEVEMENTS AND MIRACLES

Most people go through life without ever discovering the existence of that whole field of endeavor which we describe as second wind.

Katharine Graham

During my awareness, achieving and coasting periods of life, I had little time to appreciate what I accomplished. Back then at the end of each day, I might have had trouble recalling what challenges I had achieved since getting up in the morning. That isn't so when I'm enjoying being old.

The first thing in the morning, my achievements begin with my rolling out of bed by myself. Often this is a something to be admired. Throughout the day I marvel at what I can achieve. As my balance has gone out the window, by the end of the day if I haven't taken a tumble, that's a major accomplishment.

When there are more things I can do than things I fear trying to do, I am ahead of the game.

My thought inventory at night includes acknowledging at least one miracle I have been blessed with during the day. It's unfortunately that believing in miracles has gone out of fashion; but perhaps it has never been in fashion.

To confirm my belief in miracles which are not relics of the past, I appreciate the supernatural. It is good to be aware of invisible life. As committed materialism kills the possibility of a miracle, I say "yes" to the unknown. I like to give credit to the source, and some days God sprinkles miracles as if from a pepper shaker.

I enjoy being open for surprises, and if I expect miracles, they will happen. That confirms my TMBOOE claim. It is fun staying where the windmill meets the wind.

Change from "I can't to I can!"

All too soon, we become members of the herd. We learn herd rules, herd regulations, herd morality, herd ethics. Then the herd no longer leaves us when we get older. We are on our own. We have served our purpose.

THE CATERPILLAR AND I

*You are not a drop
in the ocean.
You are the entire ocean
in a drop.*

**Rumi
(13th Century Persian poet and Sufi mystic)**

The caterpillar and I have much in common. We both have four seasons of life, and we share many of the same concerns. We agree that the last stage of life can be made the best when we flap our wings and take off.

The caterpillar begins his green Awareness life when he hatches from an egg. For nourishment, his first act is to eat his egg shell. This relates to a baby's dependency upon adult caring. A newborn prospers with a lot of loving concern.

As with us humans, the caterpillar's second stage of yellow Achieving is the longest period of his life. During this go-do-get stage, he learns how to crawl on certain branches, which plants to eat, and how to protect himself. At my early age, I discovered how to walk, which foods I needed and how to stay away from danger.

To discourage birds from eating him, the caterpillar develops spikes on his back, some of them poisonous. In a flash he can change colors and roll into a tight red ball. For his rippling getting around, he has five pairs of short agile legs.

To stay alert and aware of the world around him, he has six eyes. On his three inch soft body he develops a hard head with a large mouth for his voracious chewing leaves. Like a hungry teenager, he has a constant appetite.

During my yellow Achieving stage, I worked to provide for now and for the future. I protected myself by being cautious and avoiding unnecessary dangers. For certain risks, I bought insurance.

In his blue Coasting stage of life, the caterpillar goes through a fantastic change of life. Filled with much nourishment and experience during his yellow Achieving period, he plans for his final stage of life by making a brown cocoon in which he will seal himself inside and let nature take its course.

With awe, we can imagine the transformation that takes place inside that cocoon. In this passive stage, the caterpillar's chunky five sets of short legs now become two pair of thin legs that can cling. His hard head and chewing mouth now have compound eyes, long antennae and a coiled tube-like proboscis for sipping nectar food from flowers.

Four wings develop in the caterpillar's back, all covered with colorful, iridescent scales in overlapping rows, with patterns that rival a beautiful sunset. These are attached to the thorax mid-section. When activated, some wings can fly up to 30 miles per hour.

My blue Coasting period also was preparation for my last stage of life. Having completed my yellow Achieving stage, I redirected my life. I enjoyed much travel, learned about others and expanded my interests. I prepared for the next phase of life.

When the caterpillar reaches his final purple Giving Back stage, he eats his way out of his cocoon, stretches and activates his new body. Then he is ready to test his wings and make his first flight. He is set to begin the best phase of his life with newness, exploration and enjoyment.

Instead of being earthbound and limited in range of movement, the butterfly can enjoy an aerial view of life and greatly expand his area of being. He takes pleasure with the nectar of life and gives delight to everything and everyone. The caterpillar agrees with me that the last stage of life can be made the best.

We both love being old!

MY EX-CON DAYS

Men are not prisoners of fate,
but only prisoners of their own minds.

Franklin D. Roosevelt

While reveling in my abundance of years, I remember in 1964 when President Johnson announced his War on Poverty. The local government agency working on this program asked me to solve their problem of finding employment for former prisoners. As a blanket dishonesty bond denies coverage for a loss caused by an employee with a prison record, employers had an excuse not to hire an ex-con.

I had burned experience from exposure with a jail bird when I sponsored sixteen-year-old Ronnie, an inmate at a local federal prison for juveniles. I was very pleased because I recently paid $2,000 for my new blue Chevrolet convertible. Then one day spring day when the cherry blossoms were in full bloom, I left Ronnie in my new car at my office, while I went upstairs to get something. When I came down, I found Ronnie and the car gone.

During my next two no-car weeks, my friends enjoyed kidding me with a popular radio commercial jingle from the automobile company. It was "Enjoy the USA in your Chevrolet". When they sang it, they emphasized the "your".

There was a pleasant ending to this event when police picked up Ronnie for a traffic violation, while returning from his ride to the West Coast. I regained my car, and Ronnie and I retained a close relationship after he finished his jail sentence. He died ten years later from an unexplained cause.

From this experience I knew that an ex-con could con anyone, other than another ex-con. I conceived the idea of an organization for ex-cons, completely run by ex-cons. They would approve membership and provide their members' employers with a bond covering a loss up to $250,000.

I realized that an ex-con had experienced years of having little say-so in his life. Constantly, he **had** to do this and **had** to do that. So for the organization, I planned this creed:

I want to improve myself;
I want to help others;
I want to improve the world;
And, with God's help, I will do it.

Later, at the beginning of each Bonabond meeting, I would tingle when I was hear a room, filled with husky ex-cons, begin the meeting by chanting the creed.

The local government agency approved my plan and gave me an ex-con with whom to test the program. He was Petey Greene, a thirty-year-old, wearing a loud orange shirt, who had recently been released from prison. I had read a news account of his act in prison when a fellow prisoner had climbed a tower in the compound and threatened to jump to his death.

The news reporter wrote that Petey told the warden he could rescue the man if he would then give him an instant release. The warden agreed. He climbed up and convinced the prisoner to come down, and the next day he walked out of jail a free man.

In our first meeting, I told Petey how impressed I was in knowing about this incident. I said, "It's amazing that it only took you five minutes to talk the man to come down."

He gave me one of famous toothy smile and said, "Yes, but it took me five months into talking that dude to climb up there."

I had named the new organization "Trustworthy, Inc." Petey said he didn't like the name. He said, "If you is trustworthy, you don't have to say you is. And if you say you is, you ain't."

"So," I said, "what do you suggest?"

He thought a moment, and said, "We is bonding dudes, so let's call it Bonabond."

"How do you spell it?"

Petey shot back, "I thought it up. You spell it."

Several years later when *Time* magazine did an article about Bonabond, they said I had designed it with a little from the Boy Scouts, a little from Alcoholics Anomalous and a little from fraternity life.

My largest challenge was to write a special fidelity bond and find an insurance company to underwrite it. I was turned down by a dozen companies until a vice-president at Aetna Insurance Company accepted it. I later discovered he had a brother who was a Salvation Army officer.

Our bonding experience was miraculously good. We never had to pay a claim. There was one incident when a Bonabond member first resigned, not wanting to give the organization a bad name because of what he was planning to do. He was manager of a neighborhood theatre. Tormented by his bills, he quit his job and came back one night to steal $200 from the cash register.

The theatre manager was so impressed by the honesty in the man's crime that he didn't make a claim against the bond. Two days later, he re-hired him as his manager. And the Bonabond board ignored the ex-con's plan to resign.

Petey and I struggled with organizing Bonabond. We had a board of directors that supervised the activities and approved membership. I was the only non ex-con at our board meetings, and at one session, the secretary read her notes from the previous meeting. I had recommended we request adequate funds for office supplies before the end of the federal fiscal year.

It read: *Mr. Jagoe said we got to steal as much as we need for supplies before it is too late.* I had a change made in the wording.

As the concept of a board of directors was foreign to my ex-cons, I got several business friends to attend our meetings. The ex-cons learned the meaning of works like *asset, liability, corporate responsibility* and *judicial action.*

My business friends took delight in learning ex-con language. For example, *that dude jumped over the moon* meant the ex-con had made parole on first try. And *out on the street, your bells is ringing* was a warning that you are getting a bad reputation.

At the first meeting of my friends with the board, Joe Riley, a bank president, told Petey, "We are here merely as observers."

Petey, who was looking forward to guidance from my business leaders, told him, "Joe, man, you listen to me. Out in Hollywood, when they was going to train Lassie, did they bring in another dog?" Joe laughed and got the message.

I was delighted with the warm friendship that developed from my friends with the ex-cons. Sometime later, Petey stopped by to see Charles Schwartz, one of the advisors and a leading jeweler in Washington. While they were visiting, Petey said, "Charley, man,

I like you, and I'm going to show you how I can steal any piece of jewelry I want and you won't know it."

To the jeweler's astonishment, he demonstrated how he could do it with ease. Later, with Petey as his advisor, Charley redesigned his showroom.

I learned that shop-lifting was a way of life for an ex-con. One morning in the early fall when the leaves in the park were turning red, I happened to meet Petey on a downtown sidewalk. While we were talking, I complimented him on the handsome green suede sport coat he was wearing. Petey said, "You like it? What size you wear? Stay here fifteen minutes and I'll get one for you."

I thanked him but said I was in a hurry.

During the next few years, Bonabond had served its purpose and phased out. However, the Aetna bonding program was continued and expanded nationwide by the Labor Department as the Federal Bonding Program. In 1994, twenty-eight years later, a report stated there was 99.6% success rate for 31,000 ex-cons who had found jobs though the program.

In the following years, Petey became a local celebrity with his popular TV show, *Petey Greene's Washington*. He did many good things for the community before he died of bad health in 1984, at age 53. At his funeral, the crowd filled the church with an overflow onto the street.

As if were yesterday, I remember when Petey and I went down to the U. S. Labor Department to get the $250,000 check which was to fund the program. We sat in a small office facing a little government attorney who toyed with the check in his hands.

He said, "I have studied your Bonabond organization and approve except for one thing."

We held our breath, and he said, "In your creed, you use the word "God", and we believe in separation of Church and State. So, unless you take out the word "God", I don't approve your project."

My heart sunk, but Petey gave a quick response which jolted the attorney. He shoved the check at us and left the room.

What Petey said was, "I'll tell you what, Buster. You take the word 'God' off the dollar bill, and we'll take it off our creed."

GUT

The future is in God's hands, but He assigns roles.
Discover yours and be prepared to play it well.

Voltaire

While enjoying old age, I realize I am distractible and find-ing moments to engage in contemplative thinking can be a challenge. I like the story of a man riding on a horse with a monk, and he offered the holy man the horse if he could give fifteen min-utes of concentrated prayer. The monk took the offer, hopped off the horse and knelt in silence with head bowed. Ten minutes later, he looked up and said, "Does that include the saddle?"

During the first three phases of my life with concerns mostly for the day, I had little thought about self-actualization and fun-damental questions of life. I love being old because I have time to look at myself, to be sure I am in a rightful place and to wonder if my existence might have a supernatural goal. In searching for meaning, I realize I can make a difference, and I want to find and become the person I was born to be.

I strongly agree with Paul Irving. As chairman of the Center for the Future of Aging at the Milken Institute, a think tank that studies older age, he said, "One of the great opportunities we all have is to continue that search for meaning, that aspiration to do our most enjoyable and important work later in our lives."

When I was giving a class at American University on the subject of "Self-Discovery", at the first meeting I gave the assignment for each student to write his GUT statement.

This is one's <u>G</u>reat <u>U</u>nified <u>T</u>heory, stating why a person thinks he exists. As a key that can unlock the riddle of one's life, it should be limited to thirty words. Only that person will ever see this statement, which he is to acknowledge and date every week.

In some ways, determining your GUT statement is like the scientists who have built a huge underground collider in the attempt to discover the Higgs bosom particle, which they think is the missing link to understanding the universe.

At the end of the ten week class, a woman student told me, "I hate you. You have made me feel insecure because I have not been able to write my GUT statement. I can't realize the necessity of my existence."

I was speechless. Then I told her not to give up and to keep trying to discover her reason for being. With compassion, I saw her as a rudderless boat floating in the sea.

A study was made of the natives on the Nicoyan Peninsula in Costa Rica to understand why they lived so long. A probable answer was that each had what they called a *plan de vida*. Impressed by these findings, Dr. Robert Butler, the first director of the National Institute on Aging agreed that being able to define your life meaning adds to your life's expectancy.

Even with a close friend, asking him if he has a GUT usually disturbs him. I cherish mine, and I review and date it every Monday morning. This helps to keep me on course and gets my week off to a great start. I sense I am walking on air against my better judgment.

To confirm a universal concern for some of our world hurtings, on the top of my today's schedule, I jot those for whom I will offer up that day. I never run out of subjects, such as prisoners, victims of war and revolt, refugees, abandoned children, the hungry and thirsty, and those with physical or mental illness.

From my youth, *Invictus* has been one of my favorite poems.

Out of the night that covers me,
black as the pit from pole to pole,
I thank whatever gods may be
for my unconquerable soul.

It matters not how straight the gate,
how charged with punishment the scroll,
I am the master of my fate:
I am the captain of my soul.

HAVING FUN

If you obey all the rules, you miss all the fun.

Katherine Hepburn

Being old, it is good sport to liven up each day with humor. As long as I am entertaining, listeners don't care whether or not I'm telling the truth. Most people have a low expectation of happiness, and we are the only species who laugh or need to. TMBOOE thrives on fun.

I need to prove I'm human by laughing at me with a sense of seeing myself from the outside. Robin Dunbar, Ph.D., an Oxford psychologist, said, "You should be laughing until it hurts, as opposed to a slight titter."

Norman Cousins devoted a book to his own experience of curing himself from a debilitating undiagnosed disease. Minimizing the healing power of medicine, he concentrated on humor. He spent hours laughing at old Marx Brothers movies.

Often when I feel bogged down with activities, I remember and laugh over what my childhood cook used to say. Eunice was quite a philosopher. She would put her hands on her hips and say, "The trouble in life is that it is so daily."

One of the things which used to annoy me was a telephone solicitation. Then I figured a way to make it fun. With my name "Armiger Jagoe", the person calling has a tough time trying to sound familiar. The soliciting calls begin with: "Hello, Armi," or "Hello Mr. Jargo – or Mr.Jagoeey."

This is a typical call:

(me) Who's calling?
(caller) This is Sam Thompson, with the Montgomery County Society for Police, Firemen, Orphans and Lonely Women.
(me) I know you.
(caller) *after a pause*, You do?
(me) Yes, what did you do with little Oscar?
(caller) I don't understand.
(me) Yes, you do. You took little Oscar for a walk and didn't bring him back.
(caller) *sputtering*, I think you might be mistaken.
(me) No, I'm not! I want my dog back, and you better return little Oscar, or I'm going to call the police.
(click)

Recently, at a symphony, I was in a slow moving line to reach the ticket-taker. A woman with dark red dyed hair kept bumping into me as if she were pushing a stalled car. After the fourth nudge, I turned and said, "As you are in such a hurry, I insist you go ahead of me."

Startled, she said, "No, I'm not in a hurry."

"Yes, you are," I said as I insisted she get ahead of me.

Ten seconds later, I said in a quiet voice, "Which of the two of us do you think will die first?" Her face went blank. I imagined her thought was, "You will because you are old --- but who knows?"

During the concert, I chuckled to myself, thinking this good nudging woman was spending more time thinking rather than listening.

An annoying thing in social life is a receiving line. For that reason, I have fun spooking them. I remember a wedding reception when I told each of those in the receiving line, "I just killed my mother." And I was greeted with nods, gracious smiles, and no eyebrows were raised. Reactions were:

"How kind of you."
"Thanks you for coming."
"Yes, it was a lovely event."

In 1965 my wife, Eva, and I were invited to a reception at the State Department. It was a rainy night and I let her at the building entrance and told her to go into the event while I looked for a place to park the car.

When I later arrived, I was at in a long slow-moving line, waiting to be greeting by Dean Rusk, Secretary of State. I was surrounded by State Department people talking about exotic places where they had served. I felt like a rabbi at a pig-roast.

I had time to consider what name I would give when being introduced. My first thought was "Josephus Eisenhower." But by the time I neared the first of the line, I changed my mind.

When the official greeter asked if he could give my name, I told him, "Joe Jones." He then turned and said to Secretary Rusk, "You next guest is Joe Jones."

The dignified gentleman, whom I had seen before, grabbed my hand as if I had saved his life in a past adventure. "Joe," he exclaimed, "how great it is to see you again."

"You have never looked better," I lied. "You haven't changed a bit since I saw you last. No one has ever admired you more than I do."

"Joe," he said, beginning to get emotional, "you are as kind and thoughtful as ever. I'll never forget what a treasure you have always been."

Turning to his wife, a gracious woman in a yellow dress, he said, "Dear, do you remember Joe Jones?"

Mrs. Rusk cocked her head to one side and looked at him as if he had asked if she could remember her maiden name. "Why, you silly man! Of course, I remember Joe Jones. How are you, my dear?"

"I am fine, and you look as lovely as ever. I am sorry that Brunhilda couldn't come, but she has a bad cold."

Mrs. Rusk frowned and said, "Well, you give her my love and tell her the party won't be the same without her."

Later at the reception when I located Eva, I told her, "Mrs. Rusk thinks your name is Brunhilda."

The next time I could have fun was on a crossing on the QE2. At the Captain's Reception, we stood in line while the Captain's attractive social secretary in a slim blue dress introduced him to the guests. When she asked for my name, I said, "Adamverkowskitonivich."

The smile on her lovely face froze. Her eyes crossed. Hesitatingly, she said slowly in a deep voice, "Would you mind repeating that?"

"Surely," I said. "It's Knovichtonslykovich"

She remained comatose. Then a minute later, she recovered and in a gracious tone said to the Captain, "May I introduce you to --------------- this lovely couple."

KNOW THYSELF

I said to my friend, Rabbi Jonathan Eichhorn,
"I think 64% of people go through life without
discovering themselves."
He shot back, "You're wrong! It's 92%."

I realize I have lived in many different levels, and I have the gross weight of my past life in my hands. To understand the mysteries of self and to know who I am today it's good to renew acquaintance with the persons I have been. I am a composite of the many people. As Winston Churchill said, "We shape our dwellings, and afterward our dwellings shape us."

It is refreshing to meet myself in different parts of the past. When old, instead of planting another sapling, I can enjoy wandering through the woods, now bare, I have cultivated over many years. There I rediscover hidden treasures and encounter several of my former beings, some who might seem only vaguely familiar. When I find one, I record an incident, moment of humor or something special about this person. For example, on a clear day while walking through my woods, I meet many former me's.

Me – the kid

I see a happy youngster, sitting on a log, examining a rock in his hand. An unusual thing about this boy was his love for animals. At various times during his childhood he had as pets a dog, cat, rabbit, horned toad, turtle, flying squirrel, bat, seagull, snake and opossum.

One night when a man in town shot a opossum, he found a baby in its pouch. Knowing the Jagoe kid liked anything that breathed, he gave him the baby opossum. For the next year, Sammy, the opossum, lived in a box under the boy's bed, grew larger and had the run of the house.

One spring afternoon, when the magnolia tree in the side yard was in full bloom, Catherine Harrison, daughter of U.S. Senator Pat Harrison, stopped by on her honeymoon with her California husband. The boy's mother was visited with them in the living room, when she went into the adjoining library to answer a phone call.

While talking on the telephone, she heard Catherine scream, "There is a big rat coming down the stairs!"

The boy's mother called, "No, dear, that is just a opossum." When she finished the call, she returned to the living room. There was no one there.

Me - the teenager

During his skinny teens – green and carefree, his only sad time was during the Depression when, to support the family, the father took a government job in Washington. The family was then together only for a summer month and at Christmas. Many times the kid cried secretly in his room.

Since he was twelve, he had a job, first as a newsboy. Next, he earned $.10 an hour as assistant to the two soda jerks at Grant's

Drug Store. When he reported to work, his first chore was to kill the rats trapped in a cage in the back of the store. He would drown them in a water tub in the alley.

An incident he clearly remembered happened one hot summer day when many women walking along the beach carried parasols. He was working back of the counter and every stool was filled. A dignified Negro man came to the end of the counter and asked the boy for a glass of water. He was glad to give it to him, and the man thanked him as he returned the empty glass.

Three minutes later the kid was surprised to see Mr. Wimpton, the cashier, come back of the soda fountain and grab him by the shoulder. He shouted, "Which glass did you give that colored man?" He then took one of the glasses from the rack to be washed and smashed it on the floor.

The boy was puzzled by this until closing time when Mr. Wimpton took him aside and said, "Now, kid, don't get your butt up between your shoulders. I had to do what I did because if word got around that Grant's was serving black customers, we'd lose all our business."

The boy said, "But he was thirsty."

Mr. Wimpton thought a moment. Then he said, "Next time, give him water in a paper cup."

Me – college days

In my woods, I scarcely recognize a lanky boy climbing on a tree branch. In 1939 Harvard was anxious to get students from the south and west. So, they agreed from these two parts of the county to accept without an entrance exam any boy who was in the highest seven in his class. As a high school graduate, he was #9, but since he was dating the superiendent's daughter, grades were subjusted and he became #7.

He liked everything about Harvard, except academia. He had joked his way through high school and occasionally double-dated with his teachers. This didn't seem to work at Harvard. He was on and off probation as often as he hopped the subway.

From his small southern hometown, he found Boston to be fantastic. He visited his first art gallery, attended symphonies, was on a national champion crew, got his flying license and was a volunteer cheerleader at football games. World War II came just in time for him to leave college with his head high and grades low.

Me - preparation for war

Next to a cluster of trees in my woods, I see a cocky young fellow who was convinced he was to be an important person in winning the war. He joined the Army Air Corps as a glider pilot and did his training in Tucumcari, New Mexico, where there was plenty of arid land for them to practice their unique stunts.

Flying in 85 hp. Piper Cubs, the procedure was for the instructor to cut the switch when they were at 1,000 feet and let the student make a dead-stick landing. When the wheels touched the ground, the instructor would turn back on the switch and they'd take off to do it again.

Suddenly, the powers-that-be realized how impractical gliders were in warfare, and the future glider pilots became needed bombardier-navigators, known as bombagators. Training in Albuquerque, he was one of a three-man unit, and they became close friends.

One was Jake Jacobs, a big klutzy fellow whose goal was to be a walking postman in Los Angeles. The next year, when Jake was assigned to a bombing squadron in Italy, he hitched a ride to find his close friend, who was based in Corsica. One cold winter day when his old buddy was bundled up in his tent, Jake burst in, jumped on top of him with a bear hug and the cot collapsed.

The other trainee partner was Lee Hornsby, from Alum Creek, West Virginia. After the war, Lee brought his bride to Washington to see his war-time friend, who took three days to show them many sights, from the Capitol to Mount Vernon.

At the end of their stay when the host was driving them to the bus station, he asked what had impressed them the most. After whispered together, they gave their answer. It was the hot fudge sundae at Marriott's Hot Shoppe.

Me – combat missions

When encountering this flyer in my woods, I can't grasp his never for a moment having feared the next mission to be flown. Although those in his squadron bonded stronger than kinship, it was an unwritten rule that when someone was killed or shot down, one never mentioned his name again. Perhaps they achieved this behavior by getting roaring drunk every night at the officers' club when there was no mission scheduled for the following day.

The club was a large second floor room in one of the few buildings in the area. They constructed a bar at one end, and there was a blank wall where they signed their names. The day they were to celebrate the opening of the club, our commanding officer panicked when he found the ice plant in the closest town was shut down. He had invited the general for this event.

Young Lt. Jagoe thought he had a solution. While hiking through the area, he had found a spring with very cold water. So, the commanding officer gave him his orderly and his jeep to take the bottles of whiskey and wine to soak in the spring.

They succeeded in having cool bottles, but they hadn't realized the labels would have washed off. That night during the successful inauguration, he sat on the floor beneath the bar and the fellows serving the drinks would give him each newly-opened bottle to sip and identify. Although he didn't have the chance to be social, he got soused.

This young fellow, who craved danger and was at ease with fear in flying 74 missions, is a total stranger.

Me - civilian life

Leaning against a tree in my woods, I see a tall, thin fellow who has changed from years of wearing a kaki uniform to a suit, coat and tie. He reminds me how tough were the first few months of civilian life when he was silently screaming inside and often went to sleep, hoping he wouldn't awake.

Eventually, he enjoyed the next three years working for the Hartford Insurance Company, then the second largest insurer in America. There he taught classes, travelled and absorbed corporate life. Wanting to start his own business, he left the Hartford with $1,500 in savings and returned to start a one-man operation in Washington, D.C.

Success came so gradually that he later couldn't understand how it happened. He was extremely fortunate. It was a learning experience, finding out what his potential clients wanted and developing a splendid team of employees who shared their corporate creed. It was an enjoyable time.

Me - improving the world

Sitting on a boulder in the middle of my wooded area, there is an impatient young man, wanting to change things for the better. He headed a study to evaluate public funds spent for child welfare in the District of Columbia. He was blessed with a splendid group of volunteers, and they met regularly until they completed the study twelve months later. Katherine Graham, the attractive wife of the publisher of *The Washington Post*, was one of his best chairpersons.

Me - the society fellow

In my woods, I vaguely recognize a grinning dapper fellow, getting ready for a night on the town. During the 1950s in Washington social activity and political life were closely intertwined. Those were the days of statesmen, when money was not the number one concern of both political parties.

The New York Times wrote an article about the important role of social life in the nation's capital. About the two most prominent and rival hostesses, it said Perle Mesta served more caviar than did the Russian Embassy, and Gwynn Cafritz poured more champagne than did the French

In an issue on Washington, *Cosmopolitan* magazine featured him as a popular bachelor. One evening when he and his date walked into the formal dining room through a hallway with two men servants standing erectly, he was surprised to hear a shrill sexy whistle. His first thought was that one of the servants appreciated his date in her slinky black evening gown. After dinner, when they walked back through the hallway, he discovered that the catcall whistle had come from a black Mino bird there in a corner cage.

Me - side jobs

Ignoring that his nephew was struggling to build his own business, his uncle, who was a close friend of President Eisenhower, volunteered for him to supervise the Gettysburg farm that Eisenhower had purchased. This required his going every two weeks to meet with Ivan Feaster, the capable young fellow who was farm manager.

One summer day when the asphalt road felt soft underfoot, Ivan greeted him with a legal notice, shutting off the telephone because of lack of payment. He and Ivan met with the attorney for the phone company in his walk-up second floor office on Main Street.

There, sitting behind his battered desk, the chunky little attorney nervously ran his finger inside his collar and said, "I got a problem. I'm Chairman of the Republican Party for Adams County, and I don't want word to get out that I've cut off the President's phone." The problem was solved when they found there two telephone companies in Gettysburg, and Ivan had been paying the wrong one.

On another occasion when he got to the farm, he found a dozen farmers leaning on the corral, gaping at a Brahmin bull someone had given the President. They were chiding Ivan saying, "Ole Ivan, he scared of that bull."

Ivan whispered to him, "I ain't scared of that bull. But he shore is ugly." He agreed.

Me – Eva

I hardly recognize a lucky fellow near the edge of my woods, ready to begin a splendid new phase when two lives became one. Just in time, at age thirty-eight, he began sharing his life with the person he adored. Newness included his own home, babies and diapers, a lawn mower and a garden.

With his ten thumbs he attempted to become "Mr. Fix-It". One morning, his five-year-old son, playing in the yard, heard a loud voice from inside the house. He said, "Let's go in and see what Daddy is god-damming."

There are many additional "me's" that followed. However, these are the more important ones, which I'll submit with my TMBOOE application.

> *He goes around concerned more than usual*
> *about time, life, other minor things like being,*
> *dying without having found himself.*
>
> *Juan Gelman*

THURSDAY IS AN ORANGE DAY

*There is no a single blade of grass,
there is no color in this world
that is not intended
to make us rejoice*

John Calvin

To be aware of and appreciate my world, I attach a color to each day. And that day, I try to be alert to that particular color. These are my colors:

MONDAY   green

TUESDAY   yellow

WEDNESDAY   blue

THURSDAY   orange

FRIDAY   red

SATURDAY   purple

SUNDAY   all colors

Practicing my color-for-today exercise is fun. I am often surprised and delighted to see something I might have missed. My observing sparks appreciation, which is grace of the moment. I find that color awareness can become my lookout for the presence of wonder.

One Saturday evening, my wife and I were attending the opening of a play in New York. During intermission we walked to the balcony and looked down at the other theatre goers below. I suddenly remembered it was Saturday and I hadn't seen anything purple. So, my wife and I studied the people below, and we found our answer.

There was a little woman all dressed in purple, with purple dress, purple hat, and purple shoes. She was a vivacious person, talking to those around her. And she was smoking a small pipe.

Many years later when giving a workshop, I mentioned this experience in the Broadway theatre. Later a man in the group told me, "You have seen my aunt."

Then he explained that his aunt in New York never missed the first night of a play and she only wore purple. Then he added, "Yes, and she smokes a pipe."

HOW DO YOU DO, MORTALITY

I'm not afraid of dying;
I just don't want to be there when it happens.

Woodie Allen

It's been said that happiness is like a butterfly. When pursued, it is always beyond our reach. But when one sits quietly, it may alight upon him. I take delight in relaxing and taking life in both hands to give it a good embrace.

While basking in old age, I know that 50% of happiness is determined genetically. I enjoy being healthy and skinny, caused by my having good genes. Fortunately none of my ancestors had major physical or mental ailments. TMBOOE, that's me.

40% of happiness comes from things that occurred. Winston Churchill said, "The longer you can look back, the farther you can look ahead." So, good inheritance and clear memory of the past fill most of my space for achieving happiness.

I use my 10% balance for grabbing happiness by facing mortality with both hands. It's a challenger to put my mind before the mirror of eternity. I discovered that finding inner peace can be the ultimate of happiness. Psalm 30 gives me good advice

> *Lord, let me know my end,*
> *and what is the measure of my days.*
> *Let me know how fleeting my life is.*

Like most of us, I am a procrastinator when it comes to facing mortality. Confirming that I am a migrant through time, I put my date of birth in the computer and find that I have been on earth 33,613 days. As I would enjoy living at least to age 96, this will give me 162 more days to go. Each Monday when I initial my GUT and goal statements, I add seven to the past days and subtract seven from the "to go" number.

My older daughter was shocked by this. She said, "What are you going to do when you run out of time to exist?" I assured her I can push forward that gateway to a future life. When I reach the lowest number of days left, I have a renewable option to add another 365 days.

I like how Queen Elizabeth is planning her final act. She has designed the minutest details from the guest list, flowers, readings and music selections, and to which regimental units would participate and the color of their uniforms.

My goal is to die without medical assistance, and to drop dead in a pub. In the five seconds before I hit the ground, I hope to say two words, "Thanks—and DAMN!"

Edith Stein (later known a St. Teresa Benedicta of the Cross) wrote before she died at Auschwitz in 1947:

> *I do not see very far ahead,*
> *but when I have arrived*
> *where the horizon now closes down,*
> *a new prospect will open before me,*
> *and I shall meet it with peace.*

MY FRIEND RITA

Man never legislate, but destinies
and accidents happen
in all sort of ways, and
legislate in all sorts of ways.

Plato

One of the enjoyments of being old is having time to take a front row seat and be amused, watching a re-run of unusual situations in which I found myself. This is one of them.

One winter day when there was two inches of snow on the ground, my accountant and close friend called to let me know his brother, whom I had never mct, had died. It was clear he wanted me to attend the funeral because he gave me the time and place of this event. I felt obligated to go.

In preparation, I called the Catholic Church where the funeral was to take place. A pious sounding churchwoman gave me complicated and confusing directions, ending with this ominous prediction, "You can't miss it – a church on the top of a hill."

That cold morning, I carefully followed the directions and ended on a dead-end street in a residential neighborhood. I quickly retraced my steps and tried again. Finally, I saw a Catholic church on a hill, with a hearse at the front door. I pulled into the parking lot and hurried into the church.

My wearing a dark topcoat, the usher thought I was a member of the family. He led me to a seat, next to the casket and directly behind the two front rows filled with next-of-kin. On the hard floor, our footsteps resounded like we were German storm troopers. The Mass was in full swing, and the church was smoky with incense.

With lowered head, I quickly tried to transform my appearance from harried to holy. Kneeling like a devout monk, I then opened my eyes and could not recognize anyone seated in front of me.

I glanced down at the prayer card the usher had pressed into my hand. It read, "In memory of Rita Gibson. May she R. I. P." In disbelief, I reread it three times.

After the disturbance I had made by arriving late, I couldn't up and leave. I was trapped. I had to ride it out. After silently muttering several four-letter words, I took a deep breath and unbuttoned my topcoat.

Again I observed the family members. Evidently they were there because of required attendance. No one seemed to be shaken up by Rita's passing on to her eternal reward.

At that time, the priest began a lengthy eulogy. I learned that Rita had been a single woman, who possessed every virtue known to man. You name any act of charity, and Rita had done it at least a dozen times. She made Moher Teresa look like a back-slider. St. Peter was certain to give her an A+ rating when she rattled the Pearly Gates.

The more the priest told us about the dead woman next to me in her simple gray casket, the more interested I became. This little saint had made a tremendous contribution to mankind. Few realized what a great heart this woman had.

In my mind's eye, I began to see Rita clearly. Forgetful of herself, she devoted her every waking hour to helping others. Even during a blizzard, she'd wade in deep snow from house to house, serving hot chocolate with marshmallows floating on the top and a dash of cinnamon.

After a long day, she would often return home nearly naked, having given the clothes off her back to the poor and needy. When she limped down the street — probably crippled with many ailments — dogs would wag their tails, people would give radiant smiles, cars would toot their horns — all in recognition of a *truly good* woman passing by.

When the priest finished his account of Rita's life, I was blowing my nose. The man sitting in front of me offered me his handkerchief. Giving me a secret glance, the woman in the scarlet jacket sitting beside him began to sniffle.

Later, when it was time to give the handshake of peace, tears were streaming down my face. Because of my emotional state, I had become noticed. Several fellow mourners in the front rows stretched back to shake my hand.

By the end of the funeral, I had managed to get control of myself. But as I walked with the family, slowly following the casket on sweet Rita's last trip up the aisle, I came apart. Perhaps a thousand times, this angelic soul had walked this aisle; spreading joy to everyone she passed, covering up her own pains with a brave smile. By the time we got to the vestibule, I was sobbing out loud.

My grief became contagious. Children were crying because their mothers were crying. Family members took turns hugging me like a big teddy bear, and I had a kid wrapped around each leg.

Breathing deeply, I told them how wonderful Rita had been and how much the world was going to miss her.

"After the burial," one of the women said, "we hope you will join the family for lunch at my home. We'll all be there. And you are most welcome."

I promised to come, if possible. "But," I said, "if I can't, you'll understand." They nodded.

Then I hurried out of the church into the frigid winter day. Quickly, I jumped into my car and drove away before anyone could record my tag number.

I later pictured the scene when the family members were gorging themselves at the luncheon. I could hear them asking one another, "Who the hell was that old man in the black coat?"

Then a catty soul would suggest, "Do you think old pious Cousin Rita had something going for herself?"

CHANGE, STAY BUSY AND KEEP THOSE GRAY CELLS GROWING

When you're finished changing,
you're finished.

Benjamin Franklin

One time when several young business people asked me for advice, I told them, "Change, have no regrets, keep growing and stay so busy that when you die, it will take a week to cancel your appointments."

While enjoying old age, I can't over emphasize the importance of change. As the ordinary circumstances of life are resistant to change, every day I try to be a pioneer, not a settler. No two day should be the same. For example, each night before dinner I rotate my drinks,

Monday - Canadian whiskey
Tuesday – bourbon
Wednesday – rye
Thursday – Irish whiskey
Friday – scotch
Saturday – martini
Sunday – scotch mac

One week I wear brown, the next week blue. Every Monday, I switch two pictures in my office. I know that sameness is a form of poverty.

One reason people resist change is because they focus on what they have to give up instead of what they have to gain. When advising a friend about his future, I encourage a different routine which might even mean changing his income-providing profession. This I have learned through experience because I have changed careers five times.

Even though my balance has gone to hell in a handbasket, my travel walker assures that I don't have to miss anything that is different, interesting or fun. This includes book-signings, Carnegie lectures, travel and my monthly poetry, discussion and prayer group meetings.

Merely staying busy is nothing to brag about. Henry David Thoreau wrote, "It is not enough to be busy. So are the ants. The question is what are we busy about." So I try to justify my activities.

I find renewing my mind, as my fundamental resource with its 100 billion neurons and 100 trillion interconnections, is an ongoing challenge that influences every cell in the body. Not wanting to offend God, who gave me an amazing mind meant for learning, I try each day to learn something about everything and everything about something

With the wonder of ignorance, I check on a new word I have discovered in my reading, and I record it in my personal dictionary.

When someone suggested to Pope Francis that he should slow down, he said that at his stage of life, he had to move ever faster

Freud said the mind is life an iceberg, floating with one-seventh of its bulk above water. So, every 24 hours I try to move my mind a few more inches higher out of the water.

Katherine Mansfield wrote, "The mind I love must have wild places, a tangled orchard where dark damsons drop in the heavy grass, and overgrown little wood, the chance of a snake or two, a pool that nobody's fathomed the depth, and paths threaded with flowers planted by the mind."

Well said!

AWARENESS

I go by myself
to where I am supposed to be
without ever being sure
I have arrived.

Jack Lindeman

The Latin phrase, *carpe diem*, is translated into 'seize, enjoy and pluck the day when it is ripe'. In 1817, Lord Byron wrote, "I never anticipate - *carpe diem* – the past is one's own, which is one reason for making sure of the present."

Enjoying old age, I have become a missionary for the pleasure of awareness. During my earlier hustling and bustling days, I had a restricted field of vision. Now I am convinced I should ward off trivial existence by embracing awareness in our world that is too loud.

I attempt to enrich my life by integrating it with many things new and open to the invisible. I don't want to be sleep walking on autopilot and living in a dark artic attic.

Helen Keller said, "I have often thought it would be a blessing if each human being were stricken blind and deaf for a few days at some time during his early adult life. Darkness would make him more appreciative of sight; silence would teach him the joy of sound."

During the first three phases of my life, in my mind's eye, I kept my sight down to see where I was going. Now I can look up, slow down and take in the wonder and delight of beauty. Each day I enjoy the habit of Awareness, which is the mind's faculty before thought is actually present. It puts me in contact with the universe, and I see behind the curtain.

The American artist and philosopher, John Cage, said when he sees something that doesn't seem to be beautiful, he asked himself why he thinks it not beautiful. Then he discovered there is no reason. Paul Gauguin once said, "I slow down and shut my eyes in order to see."

It is good to break from a limited perspective and to be aware of our ever-changing world. I train myself not to fall into the trap of complacency, the first cousin of boredom. There are bushels of fascinating somethings outside my four walls awaiting my interest. I am convinced that whispering stones and all living things have a memory of their own. And to observe with newness is to be.

The poet, W. S. Merwin, said, "One can't live only in despair and anger without eventually destroying the thing one is angry in defense of. The world is still here, and there are aspects of human life that are *not* purely destructive, and there is a need to pay attention to the things around us while they are still around us."

Without being alert, I can be as blind as a doorknob and pass too many things without seeing them. When I was with a group on a Buddhist retreat in Japan, we had a free day in Kyoto. At dinner that night we gave an account of what we had seen.

One had identified seven birds she had never seen before. An engineer had been fascinated by the overhead electric wires on each street. Most of the women commented on what the Japanese women had been wearing. And I was the only one who had admired many bonsais. I realized we see that which is of interest.

Unfortunately, one without interests can wade through the day being aware of little. Wise Benjamin Franklin said, "People who are wrapped up in themselves make small packages."

As a gardener, my indoor plants are a source for awareness. I make a conscious decision to notice nature's beauty and unique qualities, and I have given a name to each plant. My seven bonsais are old friends—one of them is fifty-years old. Every morning I say "hello" to them and each day I let them enjoy ten hours of classical music.

In my daily alert to fresh sight I occasionally choose a subject of interest for each day. For example, I might notice the color of the eyes of those I will meet. Eyes are tailored and are as complex as their owners need them to be. If need diminishes, so do eyes.

My having given up driving has been a widening of the screen of what I see around me. For the first time there are houses, gardens and people I had not been aware of. As an observing passenger, I am surrounded by newness.

Often I challenge my hearing. It is good to be quiet and listen. One time when I took five youngsters for a walk through the woods, I had them sit in a circle on the ground with their eyes closed. I asked them to tell me what they could hear. For a good while they heard nothing. After long silence, they said:

"I hear a dog barking."
"There is a rustling of leaves – a squirrel must be nearby."
"I hear a bird singing."
"I hear silence."

It takes but a moment during the day to shut my eyes and identify the sounds around me. I might hear traffic, a horn blown and a car siren. At night, the sound and various tones of the crickets and other nocturnal things are fascinating.

Carl Jung wrote that "a young man who does not fight and conquer has missed the best part of his youth, and an old man who does not know how to listen to the secrets of the brooks, as they tumble down the peaks to the valley, makes no sense; he is a spiritual mummy who is nothing but a rigid relic of the past. He stands apart from life, mechanically repeating himself to the last triviality!"

I often take for granted my sense of smell. A blind man so sensitized his sense of smell that walking on a familiar route through his New York City neighborhood, he could tell where he was by the odor from the shops he was passing. I have been told that an expert chef tests foods not by taste, but by his nose.

With the skill of a potter, occasionally I take time to test my tactile talent. I rub my fingers back and forth on something until I sense a tingle. The hand is an area of great mystery, and each fingertip has about 2,000 receptors for touch. I shut my eyes and touch any object – cloth, metal, wood, plastics. Information travels up the nerves in my fingertip as an electrical impulse into my brain that blends it all together. Fantastic!

Speed bumps, sometime called "silent policemen", have a useful purpose. I plan into each day several awareness speed bumps and enjoy being aware of the gift of being. I love being old because my speed bumps slow me down and remind me to enjoy the scenery, even while on a detour.

Heaven is
the place where
happiness is everywhere.

Animals,
and birds sing—
as does
everything.

To each stone
"How do you do?"
Stone answers back,
"Well. And you?"

Langston Hughes

DREAMING

They say dreams are the windows of the soul—take a peek
and you can see the inner workings, the nuts and bolts.

Henry Bromel

Discovering the amazing function and value of dreaming was like finding a fortune buried in my backyard. I became aware that I spend one third of my day in the dream world, when my subconscious is actively involved in dreaming in a shore of silence.

I realized that dreaming has been appreciated for a long time. Twenty-one of the prophets in the Old Testament recorded their dreams. And two prominent spiritual leaders, Thomas Aquinas and John Newton, recorded the importance of their dreams.

The Jewish bedtime dream preparation, the *cheshbon hanefesh*, is reflective activity when one takes time to review the day and take inventory of one's soul.

Ever since Sigmund Freud did his study of dreams in the 1900's, the neurology of dreaming has been a fascinating concept with a bottomless pit for the scientific world. Also, brain imaging has provided new bases for studying the dreaming brain.

Not having time for the scientific world to agree on the complexities of dreaming, I know that dreams are harmless and beneficial for my enjoying being old. The two hours of dreaming I have every night are like the computer cleaning the hard disc during maintenance automated tasks. Therefore, I delight in taking advantage of dreaming.

To achieve the skill of dreaming and become a good dream receiver, before going to sleep each night, I follow the advice of saying to myself three times, "I am going to remember my dreams." When I half wake up in the morning, I reflect on what I have dreamed. As soon as possible, I make a note, recalling my dreams. Then, during the day, I record them in my "dreams" compartment on my computer.

There are books written about dream interpretation, but I don't care about the meaning of my dreams. I accept them as being amusing, puzzling and of interest. For example, most of my dreams are about a younger me. Also, it is true that my first home constantly becomes alive in my dream experiences.

I agree that dreams can be a mystical sense. One night, I had a vivid dream about Mr. Tom, a devoted friend and boss when I was in high school. I had not seen or talked with him for twenty years. The next morning I had a call from one of his relatives, telling me Mr. Tom had died the night before.

I love being old, because I now have time to discover and take advantage of dreaming as a process of becoming. It's healthy and fun.

LAUGHING AT ME

A day without laughter
is a day wasted.

Charley Chaplin

I love being old because through my gate of memory, I make time to hum and get a good laugh about many funny things in my life.

In the 1930s when a postage stamp was $.03, a long distance phone call was a very expensive and complicated event. You had to go through several telephone operators and the person at the other end would get a warning, saying he was soon to receive a call from the place of destination. During the years my father worked in Washington, we only phoned him twice.

When my sister received a scholarship to L.S.U., mother felt we had to consult with father. She got on the phone and talked first with Maisie, our local phone operator. With hesitation, Maisie agreed to put her in direct contact with a long distance operator.

In detail, mother explained to the operator the purpose of the call. She said that if father got notice he was to receive a call from Gulfport, he might have a heart attack, thinking something terrible had happencd. So, the cooperative operator agreed to put the call through directly.

When father answered the phone, mother said, "Hello, Honey Bunch."

My father barked back, "Who the hell is this!" For years Mother said that reply saved their marriage.

During WWII when we picked up our B-25 in Florida preparing for flying to Europe, we were instructed not to let anyone know our destination. Thinking I was clever, I wrote home, explaining I couldn't divulge my destination in Europe, and ended with "give my regards to Ingrid and Rick, and I hope the baby arrives soon."

Puzzled by this, my mother sent copies of my letter to many friends. A week later she received telegrams saying, "Casablanca, you dummy. Ingrid Bergman and Humphry Bogart as Rick."

One day after flying a mission, I was taking a shower in the latrine when I overheard our commanding officer talking to his adjutant at the wash basin. He said, "I think Jay Jagoe is the bravest man in the squadron."

I turned off the water to listen. Then, referring to my skinny legs, he said, "Anyone who has the guts to walk around all day on legs like that."

After completing fifty missions, my crew and I were given a week rest leave in Cairo. While there, my pilot Baldy and I took a tour to Memphis. When we arrived, Arab kids rush up, selling us a handful of little freshly-made blue scarabs for $.50.

As we were walking from one excavation site to another, I concealed one of the scarabs in my palm and reached down to take up a handful of sand. While Baldy watched, I said, "Look what I found." I carefully blew the sand away and there was the little blue object.

Baldy got excited and asked what I was going to do with it. I told him I would keep it as a souvenir. He was hooked and offered to buy it from me. He kept badgering me until I finally sold it to him for $20.

The prank was too good to keep. That night in a bar I confessed. It cost me much more than $20 to pay for the evening.

One of my favorites happened when I was a swinging bachelor at a dance. A middle aged couple stopped me on the dance floor.

The woman said to her husband, "I want you to meet one of the finest young men I have ever known." While I faked modesty, she went on saying what an impact I was having on the community, etc. Then she told him, "Now, dear, shake hands with Pat Deming."

I gave him an eye-to-eye firm handshake, and we resumed dancing. Pat was one of my closest friends. Later when I told him about this, we had a good laugh.

One evening, when at a conference in San Francisco, my friend Jerry, who had a false eye, and I were having a drink at the hotel bar. The lonesome bartender was listening when Jerry complained that his eyes were tired. He insisted that Jerry use his eye drops, which he took from under the counter.

He explained that these drops worked like magic and made your eyes feel young again. "I'll show you how to do it," he said, as he had Jerry lean forward and he put drops in both eyes. "Now, he said, "put your head down and wait for it to take effect."

Jerry did as told. Then suddenly his glass eye fell out and he caught it in his hand. I thought the bartender was going to faint.

Recently, at an art show put on by our local Women's Club, when I went to pay for a painting, the cashier was a husband of one of the members and a man I had never seen before. Looking at the name on my check (Armiger Jagoe), he asked me if I were related to Jay Jagoe.

I told him I was Jay's older brother. He smiled and said, "Tell him hello for me. I know him well."

When in charge of a barge trip for crippled children on the Georgetown canal, I thought I had put a friend's life in danger. To add interest to the event, I arranged for a naturalist to come and point out things to the kids. Wanting to jazz it up, I talked my friend Karl to have on a gorilla costume and, at a certain point, to jump out of the bushes.

The barge was being pulled on a very long rope by two sturdy mules and a giant-sized driver with a club walking behind them. Suddenly I realized that when Karl jumped out, it could scare the mules, and the driver might hit Karl with the club he was carrying.

It turned out I had no need for worry. When Karl appeared, there was no panic, and the kids screamed and laughed with delight. Later, I found that, while awaiting the barge, Karl had caused a traffic jam on the highway overlooking the canal. Drivers were stopping to gape at the gorilla in the tree, waving at them.

One bitter cold day in December when the trees were bare, I went to a nursing home to give poinsettia plants to a few of my favorite patients. One of them was delightful Rosemary Donahee, once a famed reporter for women's fashions. I stopped at the door of her room to ask if she wanted a red or pink plant. Robert, her big strapping Irish husband, met me and said, "Rosemary is in a coma, but we have been married over fifty years and I know exactly how she thinks. She would like the red one."

Then, in a weak voice from the bed, I heard, "Pink!"

I had many humorous happening when I was a volunteer feeder at a hospital. When I reported to work, the nurses were glad to assign me some of the old patients who were difficult to feed. My technique was to get the person talking about himself while I shoved food in his mouth.

One time when I was having success in feeding a skinny fellow, I asked, "Let me know when you have had enough to eat."

He said, "I had enough fifteen minutes ago."

Another time, the nurse told me to try feed an ancient man who refused to eat because he thought he was too old. To get his attention, I started him eating by saying I was older than he. "How old is you?" he asked.

I told him I was eighty-five. He studied me and said, "You don't look it."

Pushing food into his mouth, I asked him how old he would have thought I was. He pondered this and said, "I would guess you was eighty-four."

Tillie was a patient always assigned to me. She was a delightful little woman whose mind was on vacation. I learned to play the role of the person she thought I was. When I was her father, we would talk about her high school days. If I were her husband, I had to try and convince her I didn't have a mistress. Most of the times, I was her boyfriend.

In this role, I knew when I came to take her to the races, I wasn't to come to the door, because her mother didn't like me. I was to toot the horn. Then she would come and jump in the car.

I had to remind her to wear her little red hat that brought her luck. We could discuss how much we were going to bet. We had to leave before the last race so she could get home before her mother discovered she was out with me.

One night when I reported to work, I was standing at Tillie's door, talking to her nurse. Then I heard Tillie say to her room-mate, "Here comes that silly old man, and I have to play the game with him about going to the races."

A GENERATION WITH NO
SONGS TO SING

Words make you think,
music makes you feel,
a song makes you feel a thought.

E. Y. Harburg

I wonder what current songs today's young people will sing to their grandchildren. Their songs sound to me like musical dirges, with a beat, beat, beat, beat, beat, beat, beat, beat, beat. With rare exception, their lyrics don't excite me. If Cole Porter could hear them, he would be rotating in his grave. For example, here are lyrics from one of today's top songs:

Hey, I was doing just fine before I met you.
I drink too much and that's an issue
but I'm okay.

Hey, you tell your friends it was nice to meet them
But I hope I never see them again.

For example, it seems shallow compared to

When I hear that Rhapsody in Blue,
I'm in another world, alone with you.
sharing all the pleasures we knew
many years ago.

Today, each new song requires a flashy promotional visual aide. The hit from one of today's top singers has an accompanying video of her lying naked in bed, flashing a satin sheet back and forth. Real classy!

I love being old because I remember when radio was our chief source of entertainment, and there were perhaps twenty top bands and the same number of popular singers. There was Guy Lombardo, Glenn Miller, Harry James, Lawrence Welk with his Champagne Lady, Frank Sinatra, Patty Page, Bing Crosby, Ella Fitzgerald, Nat King Cole, Doris Day, Rosemary Clooney, and Harry Belafonte.

Today there are as many singers and song as there are waves on the beach. And they last as long as do the waves.

Seventy years ago, *Your Hit Parade*, sponsored by American Tobacco Company, was the most popular radio show. Promoting Lucky Strike cigarettes, there was a contest. You would send a $.01 postcard with your guess of what would be the top three songs next week on the Hit Parade program.

If you were right, you would receive a gift carton of cigarettes. An official with the tobacco company said their goal was to put a Lucky Strike in the mouth of every American. They did a good job in this attempt.

I agree with Jazz historian Ted Gioia, who asserted that 21st century music writing has devolved into a form of lifestyle that willfully ignores the technical details of the music itself.

My sixteen-year-old granddaughter told me, "I totally agree about lot of popular 'Top 20' or radio songs being over-produced, repetitive, similar-sounding and even vulgar a lot of the time. I must admit that I still find myself singing or dancing along sometime. I have wondered before what songs will be remembered and replayed from our generation, especially since the quality of song production is so huge and the "top hits" are constantly changing."

Smart kid.

SWEET CHARITY SANS A BITTER TASTE

*Even if it's a little thing, do something for those who have
need of a man's help, something for which you get no pay
but the privilege of doing it. For, remember, you don't live
in a world all your own.
Your brothers are here too.*

Albert Schweitzer

During my delight of old age, I like to recall the time in 1998 when my great friends, Malcolm and Eve Bund, wanted to initiate a program to get donated cars for worthy recipients. They asked me to plan with them. I had learned how difficult it is to help others without destroying their sense of dignity.

I remember, sixty-five years ago, we in the Junior Chamber of Commerce had a Christmas party for kids in institutions, and we gave each a toy. I felt that we benefited from this more than did the kids. The next year, as a change, we had a Children's Shopping Trip. We bused the youngsters to a 5-and-10 cent store, where each could spend $2 to buy what each wanted for his Christmas presents. It was very successful.

Working with the Salvation Army, I learned much about human nature. One never minimizes the value of being. Even if the sea gets rough, one clings fast to the lifeboat.

I often volunteered to work in our traveling canteen which fed the homeless in our downtown area. One night when we showed up at our designated location, a large woman in brown sloppy attire greeted me with, "You are late!"

During a tough winter when we would have below freezing temperatures, many of the homeless slept on large sidewalk grilles through which warm air was rising. One night, I sat on a grille and visited with an old man. He told me he had been a millionaire and a former governor of Texas.

When I got up to leave, he said, "I like you, mister. This here is my grille, and you are welcome to be my guest and sleep on it anytime you like."

I also learned that we think differently. Often I would visit with the center we had for unemployed men. One evening, one of my new friends there told me, "Jay, man, you stupid. Just look at you – you got on fancy clothes and a tie what is choking you, and you got to have a bundle in your wallet.

"Not me – I got it made. Tonight I have a choice of three places what got supper, and I goes depending on what they got. And at 10 o'clock, I goes to the donut place and they gives me two dozen donuts they is going to throw away. And I shares them with my buddies."

In planning Vehicles for Change, Malcolm, Eve, and I agreed it should not be a "something for nothing" program. The car recipient, recommended by a Department of Social Services, had to pay for the car and put it to good use to improve him and others.

He would purchase the car for $700, payable over a twelve month period, and have six-month protection for car repairs.

The project has been blessed by our having chosen Martin Schwartz to head the program. No other organization has had a more dedicated and capable executive leader. Marty began Vehicle for Change from a small office trailer in a used car parking lot with fifteen donated cars.

Twenty-eight years later, Vehicles for Change has provided cars for 5,300 families. In a 10,000 square foot building with eight car hoists, the employees include 34 ex-offenders in the car repair school. When they graduate, there is a list of local garages wanting to employ them with a very good salary.

Of the many success stories from car recipients, I like the one about a sixteen-year-old boy. Very excited when his single mother got a car, he said, "Oh boy! Now since Mom can drive me home from practice, I can join the high school football time."

Five years later, he called Marty and said, "Thank you again for having given Mom a car so she could drive me to practice. I just got a four-year college football scholarship."

I kid Marty about one of the early days when we had news people there for a car dedication service. Marty had told the reporters how families would use the cars for getting to work, improving themselves and helping others. Then one of the women car-recipients told the reporters, "Oh boy! First thing I'm gonna do is drive my kids to King's Dominion Amusement Park."

We laughed with approval.

REMEMBERING LAUGHTER

*Sharing tales of those we've lost
is how we keep from really losing them.*

Mitch Albom

The enjoyment of being old gives time for the reality of memory. It provides me with a lush canal in which to coast down and recall interesting events and revisit places that no longer exist.

In 1938, my mother and I drove her 1927 Packard to spend two weeks with my father in Washington. He drove back with us for his vacation on the Coast. As the old car was an oil guzzler, we had to stop every fifty miles to have it checked.

The procedure was the same. In every town we drove through my father, the driver, would insist upon finding the village idiot to confirm we were on Route #1. Mother sat on the back seat, reading Mary Baker Eddy and doing her daily Christian Science homework. At each filling station, father would get out and talk politics with the service fellow, mother would go to the ladies room, and I would buy three Cokes for us to enjoy before resuming the trip.

At one stop, we decided we didn't want a drink, so we made the time short. Fifty miles further, we stopped at a country filling station, surrounded by fields. The procedure was the same, but as father and I waiting a considerable time with the Cokes, we became concerned why mother was taking so long in the restroom. Father had the woman working there check, and she astounded us by saying there was no one in the ladies' room.

Ten minutes later, a police car pulled up with mother sitting in the front seat. For the rest of the trip, when mother went to the restroom, she took the car key with her.

During the war when I was getting bombardier training in Albuquerque, I had to fly another mission one Saturday afternoon, and I planned to meet my fellow cadet buddies later in town at the bar in the Alvarado hotel. When I arrived, the fellows were in happy mood. Seeing me, Jeff, from Highlands, N.C., shouted, "Jay, don't we have the god-damn-dest time!"

The cadet next to him whispered that his language had shocked the woman sitting next to him. Jeff turned and slapped her on the shoulder and said, "Lady, I apologize, I'm a son-of-a-bitch if I seen you there."

She looked shocked, then gave an explosive laugh and bought us a round of drinks.

Along my memory canal ride, I remember at a social event I introduce my friend, Don Punch, to one of my mother's friends. With a gracious smile, she said to him, "I am sorry, but I didn't get your name."

Don, who had had a few drinks, took his finger and poked her in the stomach, and said, "Punch!"

She gave an astonished laugh and said, "Now I have it. I'll never forget your name."

Several months later, Don and I ran into the same woman at another event. She introduced us to friends with whom she was talking. She said, "I want you to meet Jay Jagoe and his friend, Mr. Goose."

During WWII, when I was flying missions in Corsica, Don was a sergeant, serving with a photography unit in England. In his letters, he was bemoaning how unhappy he was. So, I sent him a picture to cheer him up. I had gotten it when I was on our recent rest jaunt in Cairo.

Prior to our leaving the squadron, Colonel Edwards asked me to look up Ida, his girlfriend who was working in Cairo as a civilian. He also gave me his present to give her. When we made contact, Ida suggested I take her out to dinner. I did, and when she appeared, my teeth nearly fell out. Ida was a duplicate of beautiful Betty Grable, every serviceman's pin-up favorite.

After dinner when I took her home, I asked if I could have a picture of her to show the fellows back at the squadron. She agreed and gave me a WOW! picture of her sitting on stairs with a "come hither" look, showing her beautiful legs. This was the picture I later sent to cheer up my friend in England. In appreciation, Don said he would eventually mail to picture back to me.

After I finished my missions, I returned home while Don was still overseas. When I stopped by to visit with his parents, Mrs. Punch told me that Don had a new girl-friend in London, and she thought it was a serious affair. She said, "He even sent us her picture."

With skepticism, she added, "She looks like a lovely person. Come, I want to show you."

I followed her into the living room, and there in a silver frame on top of the piano was Cairo Ida.

On the side of my memory canal, with the bank covered with purple vines, I enjoy recalling an experience my sixteen-year-old son, Louis, and I had while flying to Europe. My wife had taken the three younger children with her for our summer in Spain, and we followed two weeks later.

On the plane, Louis sat by the window, I was in the middle, and on my right was a very proper English lady, who introduced herself as "Dame Marjorie". Soon after take-off, she warned us that she was going to get violently air sick. I suggested she get something to eat, and she said she had a meal at the airport.

I had a disturbing vision of this lovely lady throwing up on top of Louis and me. So, I whispered to Louis to play along with me, and I said to my female traveling companion, "It is delightful to have you with us, but if there hadn't been an astounding criminal event in our family, my wife would be sitting in your seat."

I let this soak in. Then Marjorie said, "I don't want to appear inquisitive, but what happened?" With Louis' collaboration, we told her a cock-and-bull story that could have been a movie script. While we talked, the English lady became so interested I thought she was going to sit in my lap.

The plot was that my father-in-law had died, and they suspected he had been murdered by one of his wife's many male admirers. We stretched this tale out for half an hour. When I was laughing so hard inside that I couldn't talk, I would nudge Louis who continued the tale.

It worked. Marjorie didn't get sick, and she joined me with a gin and tonic. That fall, she submitted a recipe for a dessert cookbook my wife was writing. And on her return to the States the following year, she and her daughter had dinner with us. During the meal, out of discretion, she did not bring up discussion about the "astounding criminal event."

IF

I love being old because I have time to reflect on infinite number of important "if's" in my life. Because of them, I am alive and am blessed to have what I have and to be who I am. They inspire me for the role I enjoy playing now.

Two major "if's" happened when I was flying missions in WWII. At the last minute before my second flight, if someone had not turned in a flack helmet for me to use, my head would have been shattered when a German anti-aircraft shell crashed through the cockpit and knocked me out with a hit on the head.

On an important mission when we were bombing the target from different heights, crouched in the nose of the lead plane I saw from an upper plane a 500 pound bomb fall within 20 feet of our left wing. Had it been a fraction closer, it would have hit our plane, exploded and wiped out the covey of six planes in my squadron.

If I had not been forced, over my strong objecting, to attend a cocktail party on Christmas Day, I would not have met the attractive Spanish girl, who has become the most important person in my life. And if Eva had not chosen to visit America instead of an invitation from a friend in South Africa, she would not have been at the party.

In listing my most valued friends, I find each to be the gift of an "if". When I was in a college summer school, I was in the washroom when Professor Andrew Flagg, a fellow student, asked me why I shut my eyes when I brushed my teeth. We laughed and gradually became friends. Throughout his life, Andy became a much loved member of my family. He spent most of his holidays with us, including an enjoyable summer in Spain. If he had not initiated a conversation in the washroom, this might not have happened.

Five years ago, I was on a stool in a London pub, packed with people, noise and fun. A man standing behind me was talking loudly on his cell phone to his girl-friend who wanted his approval to buy an expensive coat. Finally I told him to give me his phone. He hesitated. When I repeated my request as a firm order, he handed it to me.

I told her who I was, and she explained she was in a department store two blocks away. I told her to put on the coat and walk to a mirror. She did. I asked her how it looked. "Beautiful," she said. When she confirmed the coat felt wonderful and that she was certain it would make her happy, I said, "Buy it, and wear it to the pub for me to see it."

When I handed the phone back to the man, he gave me a skeptical look and said, "Well, thanks a lot, mate."

Soon a beautiful Russian walked into the pub, glowing in her new coat. Today, Luke and Sonia are two of my very special friends whom I enjoy every time I return to London.

When I was chairman of the landscape committee in our condominium, we were having a meeting in the lobby and a stranger in a red striped shirt walked by. The manager told me, "There is Mark Talisman, a new condo owner, and he knows all about plants."

I asked her to invite him to join us, and I was amazed at his gardening knowledge. Before Mark got to his condo, I had called his surprised wife, telling her I was pleased that her husband was to be co-chairman of our landscape committee.

Today, Mark is my closest and most interesting friend. Each month, I look forward to our two-hour lunch. If he had not happened to be walking by the lobby on that special day, this treasured relationship would not have come to be.

The multitudes of "ifs" which have enriched my life have made me TMBOOE.

ROLL WITH THE PUNCH

Today, patience and acceptance are controls over the tempo
of contemporary life that otherwise controls us.

Regimra

I n accepting many things today and attempting to interpret the present time, I feel like a reed that bends before every wind. To avoid the shock of self-image, I think thirty-five and avoid mirrors and photographs. In the morning when I see myself in the bathroom mirror, I say, "Old man, I don't know you are, but I am going to shave you anyway."

Without consult me, they have made changes that require acceptance and achieving. I find that they have

made curbs higher,
doors stronger,
destinations further away,
print smaller,

buttonholes tight,
things get a lot longer to get done,
jars tougher to open, and often I need a child to open a
    child-proof medicine container,
coats have grown with shoulders too broad,
putting my right arm into a jacket is easy, but in the left
    sleeve is often evasive.

As another older friend told me, "These days I spend a lot of time thinking about the hereafter. I go somewhere to get something and then wonder what I'm hereafter."

With care, I merge my experienced life with a generation who feel they know more than ever before. I chuckle about the story in 1977, when for the fiftieth reunion of his historic trans-oceanic flight, Lindberg was invited by the French government for a special celebration in Paris. When he was getting settled in his plane seat and having trouble with the seat belt, the young hostess came to help him. "Mr. Lindberg," she asked in complete honesty, "is this your first overseas flight?"

Everyone is considerate of my being ninety-five, and I have learned how to react to kindness. Unless it is going to throw me off balance, I welcome a helping hand. Accepting a "may I help you?" makes the other feel good for having done a good deed.

It's alright for me to say, "If you need my help, let me know." But I never say, "I want to help." If I offer assistance I am the only one who doesn't get nervous. I remember when my feeble older sister would insist in helping to clear the table after dinner. We held our breath, hoping she wouldn't drop the dish.

I am a life-time Catholic. I have four children, their spouses and ten grandkids, most who have never seen the inside of a church, synagogue or mosque. They are good, kind, and considerate, and they have no organized religion. Although I have concern, I keep it myself. They are great kids.

Growing up in Gulfport, Mississippi, I was twenty-years old before I knew a divorced person. Today, three of my children are divorced. Two have chosen splendid second-time mates whom they probably won't marry. So, who cares? - - not I.

During my courting days, I followed the behavior pattern of my parents and grandparents. I dated many girls, took them to movies, dinners and social events. Then when I found that special one with whom I wanted to spend the rest of my life, we married and slept together.

Today, the mystic of romance is of the past. With the exception of marriage, which is a future option, those in the present generation have reversed the order. So be it.

The most radical thing I did when in high school was to get a crew cut. Today, one granddaughter has a tattoo and a ring in her nose and jewelry in her navel. Another has a diamond stuck in a nostril, one has a silver bar in her left ear and a grandson has hair below his shoulder. The one I love most is the one I have seen last.

When I listen to their music I clap even though the songs sound the same to me. Each is a beat rotation with loony lyrics. I shift into neutral and accept the current. Pardon me, Mr. Hammerstein.

Twenty-five years ago, in connection with my book, *Next in Line, Everyone's Guide for Writing an Autobiography*, I did a workshop for seniors in Florida. The next day, the only complaint was that I had often used the word "damn". Today, obscene words of the past are commonplace.

In writings, movies and TV shows, I hear these gems: ass-hole, ass-kisser, bastard, boobs, and fuck, mother fucker, piss, pissed-off, son-of-a-bitch, shit, and tits. Today, with no blush, we embrace as commonplace our inherited hushed obscenities. I doubt that the current generation has new words they consider obscene to pass on to the next generation.

Hurrah for change and a life that is filled with mysteries. I remember when bras were burned; now they are padded. Today we have information source that is the most powerful than the world has ever seen, and with my computer as a memory partner, I have no need to remember facts.

I worry that we have quit talking to one another. I recently went into a coffee shop where every seat was taken by persons humped over computer gadgets. It was as quiet as a library. I was tempted to shout, "FIRE!"

I am not concerned about my total recall occasionally becoming turtle recall. I like the story of four men, who were college alumnae and had kept in touch. Once a year, they would meet to discuss old days. When they were fifty, they decided to go to Charlie's, because the attractive women food servers wore skimpy uniforms.

For their next meeting when they were sixty, they agreed to go to Charlie's because the food was good. At seventy, they went back to Charlie's because the restroom was on the first floor. Then at age eighty, they chose Charlie's for lunch because they had never been there before.

MY BEST FRIENDS

If there are no dogs in Heaven,
then when I die,
I want to go where they went.

Will Rogers

I have always been a dog-man. Since I was five-years-old until twenty-five years ago when we moved into a condominium, I have had a dog. Enjoying being old, I have time to reflect on two of my most special best friends.

During my war days in Corsica, in a trek through the woods, I found a small German shepherd type dog that had been terrible mistreated. I took this cowardly dog back with me and named her Sally, after Axis Sally, the German radio performer who nightly would urge us to quit bombing and come join the enemy.

Sleeping under my cot in our tent, it didn't take Sally long to recover and become a very feisty animal. One day I took her with me to get something from our plane, and she suddenly rushed off, chasing a B-25 that was taxiing by. And her affection was amazing.

Her behavior confirmed what Sir James George Frazer wrote in 1890 – "things act on each other at a distanced through a secret sympathy." When I would return from an easy mission, I usually couldn't find her. But when I came back from a rough mission, as soon as I left the de-briefing session, Sally would be waiting for me and go crazy. She would whimper and keep jumping on me until I would take her in my arms and stroke her while she licked my face.

Those were the days with no radio-communication from the mission back to the squadron. When I become lead navigator, I would take Sally with us in the jeep out to our plane and leave her with the three fellows who were our ground crew. They told me they would know how the mission, 300 miles away, was going by watching Sally.

They said if the mission was easy, Sally slept quietly. But if it was a rough mission, she would start a strange behavior, whimpering and going around in a circle. When she was like this, they were afraid to get close to her. They clocked her behavior, and it always was when we were over our target.

After I finished my missions, I flew to Naples for several weeks, waiting for a flight back to the States. I was told that after I left, Sally was so despondent they planned to fly her to Naples so I could take her home with me. However, before they could do this, Sally was killed, chasing a man on a motorcycle.

Another dog I enjoy remembering was Pinto, a big Dalmatian with a large head. When we first had the dog, it was a problem because he would keep jumping through the screen door and annoying neighbors. To solve this, we made arrangements to fly Pinto to Spain, with plans for him to stay at the family finca in the country.

However, my father and mother-in-law had other plans for Pinto. They kept him close wherever they were. He became so spoiled that in the car he refused to sit up front with the driver, and insisted upon sitting in the back, between the two of them. When he was at the finca, we later learned that Pinto enjoyed exploring the area and becoming a Casanova for female country dogs.

When we would go for our summer vacation in Spain, Pinto would revert to being my best friend. He was with me constantly. Seven years later, during our visit we found Pinto was in very bad health. Rather than leaving a crippled and very sick dog for Eva's parents, we reluctantly decided to have him put to sleep.

The day the vet was to come and give Pinto the shot, when I got up for my early morning swim, Pinto limped with me down to the pool and slept on my towel while I swam. At noon, the vet came to give Pinto the fatal shot, and I held him in my lap, stroking his head until he stopped breathing. I cried.

A week later, when I opened the door for my early swim, I found a little black and white cur dog waiting for me with his tail wagging. Later, the caretaker told me that when he went to investigate a barking at the gate, this little dog ran through his legs and up to the main house. This happy little dog followed me down to the pool and lay on my towel while I swam.

Many days later, when we realized this new dog had no intention of leaving, we took him to be vaccinated. While there, we were puzzled when the vet asked us how we had been able to find one of Pinto's puppies. He then showed us the inside of the dog's back legs. There were the black spots of a Dalmatian.

DOCTOR "ME"

A few years ago I realized if I was to enjoy old age, I had to take charge of my body. I should determine the right medicines and exercise. My body knows what to do, unless my mind gets in the way.

As my mother was a Christian Scientist, the only medicine we had in our home was mercurochrome and Pluto Water, which my father thought would cure anything. Throughout my life, I had been medicine-free until I was ninety when I was a patient in a hospital because of a urinary infection. That was the beginning of real trouble.

In the hospital, several doctors convinced me I should rely on medical suppliers to be assured of a healthy balance of my life. I began taking six prescribed pills a day. A month later, I was back in the hospital with ten hours of screeching pain in my right leg.

Each hospital person who came to view me asked the same question: "When did you fall?" When the doctors found no cause or cure for my pain, I was sent home three days later with an additional prescribed medication.

Later that year, because of excruciating paralysis in both legs, I had another hospital stay. I experienced Shakespeare's King Lear lamented the tortures of aging. There was another series of "When did you fall?" questions.

The doctors were disappointed when a series of ex-rays showed no cause for pain. When I was released, the surgical doctor (to cover his ass) declared I had a splinter fracture in my hip, which would require surgery. If I had followed his advice, today I probably would be in a wheelchair. Have you ever heard a doctor or hospital say, "mia culpa"?

Being a TMBOOE person, I found a splendid doctor who agreed that I was allergic to medication. Now each day, I take two one-half medical pills, a baby aspirin and a bundle of homeopathic pills. What a joy I have in again being pain-free and feeling frisky.

I agree with an article in a medical journal which said, "Nobody has any real idea of what effects the drugs they are prescribing are likely to have on their patients. The $600 billion pharmaceutical industry develops and produces the drugs prescribed by real doctors the world over. They buy clinical trials which show bad results for a drug and publish only those that show a benefit."

When I read the label on a medicine, I find in large letters the ailment it will eliminate. In very tiny print, to protect itself from legal action, the medical producer lists about twenty possible after-effects one might experience, including death. I find this not comforting.

Regarding exercise, I had to do a mind change. For nine decades, I thought my physical well-being depended upon "more is better". Jog another block, do another push-up, work more exercise machines in the gym, swim one more lap, etc. Then new aches forced me to take physical therapy. No longer did I consider competing with Dr. Otto Thaning who at age 73 swam the English Channel.

Any object over fifty-years-old is considered an antique. Therefore, my ninety-five-year-old body is a very valuable antique, requiring special care. Producing stronger muscles is now a thing of the past, and I need exercises that will help flexibility and posture.

With good fortune, I discovered Qi Gong, which has been keeping older Chinese seniors in top shape for several thousand years. Now, with thirty minutes of seated Qi Gong each day, I keep perking along.

I have a sedimentary friend who doesn't accept my advice to do practical exercising. He told me that if God had meant for him to touch his toes, he would have put them on his knees. To support his opinion, he points out that a rabbit runs and hops and only lives 15 years and a tortoise doesn't do either and can live up to 450 years. He said that if walking is good for your health, postmen should be immortal.

To each his own.

JEWS, WOMEN, PEOPLE OF COLOR

The air is the only place
free of prejudice.

Bessie Coleman

I love being old because I have time to reflect on periods of amazing prejudice. As a TMBOOE person, nothing topples my gyro quicker than discrimination. And I have seen a bushel of it.

I credit much of the success of my company to my choice of executives. The key persons were a Jew, a woman, an African American, a Protestant and a Catholic.

Regarding prejudice against Jews, I remember where I was sitting at a U shaped table during dinner before the board meeting of our Junior Chamber of Commerce. I had nominated for the board Mandy, a close friend and member who had done an excellent job in heading a recent community project.

By accident, the person sitting beside me slipped me under the table a piece of paper which had secretly been passed around the table. It said, "Jew".

My shock was instant. Shaking with emotion, I stood and told the group that if Mandy were not approved, I was resigning. Later, the sheepish group unanimously voted his approval.

It was a man's world in 1972, when Bobbi Gibbs was the first woman to run in the Boston Marathon. There was wide spread resentment. During the race, she was attacked by a male protester.

Early in my career, I was in charge of hiring for the local office of the Hartford Insurance Company. Regardless of their qualifications, women could only be secretaries or typists. The corporate thinking was that the agents we served would not accept a woman underwriter.

In my book, *Tell It Again, Mother Goose*, I modernized the Jack and Jill rhyme.

> Jill and Jack beat off the pack,
> to climb the corporate ladder.
> As C.E.O., Jack stubbed his toe,
> and Jill was the survivor.

In my company, Layne, one of my key executives, was a very talented person, and she was gifted with quick wit. One of our major clients was Green Thumb, a government agency, which was using seniors to clean up new park areas around the country. The government employee who worked as our coordinator was Sam, a persnickety government fellow, who often tested Layne with his countless questions.

One day near closing hour, feisty Layne told me, "If Sam calls again, I'm tempted to tell him where to stick that Green Thumb."

At one time, there was not one African-American employed by an insurance company in the city. As a personal favor, an insurance manager agreed to hire an African-American receptionist, provided I selected her. A year later, she was the most popular member of his staff.

Even though I was president of the local insurance association, there were many raised eyebrows when they found I had Henry, an African-American, as one of my vice presidents.

Henry was quiet and older man who fit well into any situation. When I was having a review in my office with a client, I often would ask Henry to sit with us. Later during the meeting, I would excuse myself and leave Henry alone with the client.

Often the client would tell me how much he appreciated Henry. The comment was usually, "That was the first time I have had a serious talk with a black man."

I was amused as I shared prejudice with Henry when we would go for lunch. We were always seated at a far table, next to the kitchen. And our service was not always the best.

As a life-long smoker, Henry ended his life with many ailments. After he had been in the hospital for two weeks, he called me while he was recuperating at home. He wanted to have a private talk.

I picked him up with his walker and oxygen tank, and he directed me to drive to a park where we could talk. He began by saying, "While I was in the hospital, I had time to do some serious thinking,"

I told him I understood. He continued, "We have to realize that we don't live forever and we should make plans accordingly."

"Yes, Henry, I agree."

Then he said, "The thing that concerns me is what would happen to our company, if something happencd to you."

My splendid friend died two weeks later.

BRAVERY AIN'T CHEAP

One isn't necessarily born with courage,
but one is born with potential.
Without courage, we cannot practice any other virtue
with consistency.
We can't be kind, true, merciful, generous, or honest.

Maya Angelou

Being old, I am gifted with time to relive mentally important past heroic events and people who made them happen. I like to recall Jerry Baron. He wasn't tall; he always had a slight smile; he appreciated humor; and he was stingy with his words.

During WWII, on many of my missions, I was squadron lead navigator and Jerry was lead bombardier. The only mission we flew together was one of importance. Our target was the most feared – the Brenner Pass.

At the northern tip of Italy, this was the narrow passageway in the Alps through which Germans were sending war materials and troops. Our target there was the railway terminal. The location was a dead-end challenge for us navigators.

Normally, as soon as "bombs away!" was shouted over the intercom by the turret gunner, it was my responsibility to call for the evasive action which would get the squadron out of enemy fire and safely back to base. Normally, I had many choices – straight ahead, turn, climb, dive, right or left.

But not when we were hitting the Brenner Pass. After the bombs had dropped, we were surrounded ahead by high-rising mountains. We could only do an about-face, which gave the Germans on the ground more time to adjust their anti-aircraft guns.

In the design of a B-25 you got into the nose compartment by sliding, feet-first, through a narrow six-foot tunnel to the left of the pilots. During a mission, as navigator in the nose compartment I decided the route and timing to get to the target at a designated time.

When in range of the target, one of the gunners would drop bundles of tassel through the bomb bay. These were packaged metal shaving which would cause the first of the metal-detecting German anti-aircraft shells to explode 1,000 feet below us.

The bombardier would crawl though the passageway to join me and humped over the massive Norden Bombsight, he controlled to mission until the gunner shouted over the intercom that our bombs had dropped. The bombardier would crawl back through the passageway, and I would again be in charge.

During that mission I remember clearly the bomb run. I was, in the nose compartment crouched with Jerry, and we flew into a frightening dark cloud of shell blasts. We could smell the explosives.

During the one minute bomb run, the plane was being shaken with hits, and the sound of blasting German antiaircraft explosives was deafening. The moment after our bombs dropped, I shouted to Jerry to get out of the nose.

"No," he shouted back. "You get out! I'll take over!"

I protested and Jerry, red in the face, screamed "I'm captain and you are a lieutenant. I order you to get your ass out of here."

I scurried out the tunnel and stood back of the pilots, praying through five minutes of hell. Had we been hit, I probably would have been the one with the best chance of survival. I could have snapped a parachute to my vest harness and dropped through the open bomb bay.

We survived the ordeal and limped back to our base in Corsica with our crippled B-25. Later, our ground crew counted over 100 hits on the plane. That evening, I took Jerry aside to thank him for what he had done. He had safeguarded my life over his.

Sluffing it off, he said, "I did what I did for selfish reasons. If we got hit, I didn't want both of us scrambling to get through the tunnel."

After the war, Jerry visited me several times. Then he moved to Florida and we lost contact. But, "Buddy, today you are with me, and I love you - you lousy bastard."

OTHERS

People, who live in a society,
who enjoy looking into each other's eyes,
who share their troubles,
who focus their efforts on what is important to them and
who find this joyful—
these people lead a full life.

Albert Einstein

Fifty 90-year old seniors were asked, "If you could live your life all over again, what would you do differently". Their responses boiled down to three answers:

1. Reflect more
2. Risk more
3. Do more, especially more things that would touch other people.

I love being old because, rather than being self-centered, I have time to express my appreciation for many new and seasoned "others" in my life. I enjoy being in communion with those, both seen and unseen, who also occupy our planet. Every month I want to enrich my life by adding at least one new special friend.

Their lives spill into mine and my life flows into theirs. I have no time for loneliness with a life inhabited by strangers. Everyone is of great value. As Pope Francis said, "we should avoid physical and social walls that close in some and exclude others."

At the funeral, a woman who had been a lifelong friend of the deceased moaned to me, "Ah, the rank gets thinner." This statement haunted me for some time. Then, instead of my sympathizing with this sorrowful soul, I was critical. If her ranks were getting thinner, it was her fault. She was making herself a self-made tragedy by living among tombs.

Every day, I try to develop and increase the number of others who add value to my life. To keep in touch, I have two lists—one is for people to contact monthly, the other for those who deserve an occasionally call. Often my call might be the only one my friend might receive that day. A typical response is, "It's good to hear from you" and "It's great to be remembered!"

My others like to tell me what they have been doing, how they are feeling and what might be their concerns. With Frank, who was the flight engineer on our plane when we were flying missions during WWII, he enjoys reminiscing about the past.

The deepest principle in human nature is the desire to be appreciated. I encourage people to open up and tell me about their lives. Then, perhaps, they will become another other in my life. I willingly take a stance beneath the other person.

As I mentioned earlier, the four words that will assure you of a new relationship are: "Tell me about yourself." One who doesn't want to talk about himself is as rare as a woman not wearing jewelry. Initially one might infer aloofness, but this is usually short lived.

An incident that occurred when I was doing a workshop confirmed Ronald Reagan's saying, "We can't help everyone, but everyone can help someone." For the following week, I gave each in the group the assignment to see people with new eyes, to meet someone new and to search for the invisible "I" in others. At the next meeting, a woman in the workshop told of her unique experience.

She said, "When I was working in my front yard, I saw a woman hurrying by with a concerned expression on her face. I waved to her and said, 'Have a good day.' The stranger stopped and studied me. Then she said, 'I am hurrying to get to church, but on my way back, may I talk with you?'

"Later when she returned, I suggested we go inside to have a coffee. Two hours later, she left after we had becoming friends. It was amazing how many interests we have in common. This attractive person and I shared experiences and advice, and we are having lunch together next week."

I like to remember what Abraham Lincoln said. It was "I don't like that man. I am going to get to know him."

THANKS A HEAP

Our heritage and ideals, our code and standards - the
things we live by and teach our children –
are preserved or diminished by how freely
we exchange ideas and feelings.

Walt Disney

As the sixth great extinction has already begun, I like thinking about what is to come after I have blasted off. With concern for the future, I would like to take with me some world disturbing situations. Unfortunately, I will abandon many problems for others to solve.

In thinking ahead, I doubt I will be here to ride in a driverless car or wait for a drone to deliver my pizza. I want future generations to grow up in a world better than ours today, but there are hurting of the world I am leaving for future remedy. Many are the problems yet to be solved.

Paying under the table to get what you want has been around a long time. I bet one of my Neanderthal ancestors got the best spot in the cave by giving the head-fellow a choice slab of mastodon meat. A concern I am passed on the next generation is how to keep corruption within reasonable bounds.

We criticize bribery (def. *anything given to persuade the decision of another*) in foreign countries. Yet we accept over 10,000 Federal Registered Lobbyists with their task of lobbying, (def. *attempting to influence decisions made by government officials.*). Analyst James A. Thurber estimated that the actual number of working lobbyists was close to 100,000.

In 2015, lobbyists gave $3.2 billion in persuading their particular causes Over an eighteen year period, the U. S. Chamber of Commerce paid for lobbying $1,246 million, National Association of Realtors $353 million, and General Electric $335 million. In the 2014 elections, the pharmaceutical industry, the third rail of politics, spent $32 million in campaign contributions and another $229 million in lobbying.

Three important things about politics are money, and no one can remember the other two.

With each Congressman needing at least $5 million for his next election, the fund raiser is the most important staff member in a Congressman's office. When elected to office, a major concern of most Congressmen is their re-election. I admire the British system of limiting campaigning to three months. Ours is three years.

Those following me will have a tough time attempting to salvage our broken and feuding branch of government, and an obsolete and ineffective Electoral Congress. This is not a new problem. Eighty-five years ago, Will Rogers said, "We could certainly slow the aging process down if it had to work its way through Congress".

For the past decade, when I have asked friends to name a statesman, I get no reply. When I ask if they would like to have lunch with a Congressman, I get a shake of the head.

Regarding our national financial situation, instead of leaving a monetary bequeath to those following me, I am gifting them with a rising federal debt. If forced to pay off today, every citizen would have to cough up $42,000.

We are sitting on a powder keg filled with over 15,000 nuclear weapons in nine countries, each bomb ready to be fired. Former Secretary of Defense William Perry said, "We are facing nuclear dangers today that are in fact more likely to erupt into a nuclear conflict than during the Cold War." When the next atomic bomb explodes, I probably will be looking down from a cloud, sobbing and beating my chest.

Today, we are caught in the gap between evolution and our environmental sea change. Each year the planet breaks another global-warning record. It's going to be a tricky job one day to build a Netherland-type dyke protecting the flooding of New York City.

Living in the gun capital of the world, an American has a 6,000-to-one chance of being a terrorist victim versus being shot. After a publicized massacre by a gun man, Congress beats its breast. Then the members vote to increase the number of available guns.

In *Tell It Again, Mother Goose*, I wrote this ditty:

> Johnny had a little gun,
> and shooting it was fun.
> Sunday, he shot an ordained preacher,
> Monday, his fourth grade teacher.
> Tuesday, he shot his own first cousin.
> Wednesday, neighbors by the dozen.
> Thursday, his folks realized
> the kid should be analyzed,
> Friday, this made Johnny very mad.
> Saturday, he shot his mom and dad.

Having the world's highest penal population, someone has to remedy our prison system. With a sense of justice, we have to figure out how to rehabilitate prisoners, instead of merely warehousing and hardening them

Our division between the rich and poor is a source of embarrassment.

I end with a lament from H.H. The 14th Dalia Lama.

We have bigger houses, but smaller families,
More conveniences, but less time.
We have more degrees, but less sense,
more knowledge, but less judgment,
more experts, but more problems,
more medicines but less healthiness.
We've been all the way to the moon and back
but having trouble crossing the street to meet a new neighbor.
We build more computers to hold more information to produce
more copies than ever, but have less communication.
We become have long on quantity, but short of quality.
These are times of fast foods, but slow digestion,
tall men but short character,
steep profits but shallow relationships.
It's time when there is much in the window
but nothing in the room.
Man sacrifices his health
in order to make money.
Then he sacrifices his money
to recuperate his health,
and then he is so anxious
about the future that he does
not enjoy the present or the future.
He lives as if he is never going to die
and then dies having never lived.

HELLO OUT THERE

I thought it would be nice to make up
my mind about God,
before he makes up his mind about me.

Wallace Stevens

I find that as the body shrinks and weakens, spirituality soars. I love being old because I now have time to wonder why and what I believe in. I find it exciting to go forth from myself and try to pierce the true mysteries of God.

It is a delight to find wise writing by someone who lived long ago. In 1,386, Father Walter Hilton, with the Augustinian Priory in Thurgarton, England, wrote, "All the movements of the old man must be burned out with the fire of desire, and new feelings, the fruits of grace, introduced with burning love and spiritual light."

My go-do-get periods were crammed with being overscheduled, overcommitted and overextended. Unaware that I was a TMBOOE candidate, I was like a brown hamster in a spinning wheel, I didn't take time to stop and look at myself. When I was occupied with awareness and achieving in our civilization of diversion, I was deeply involved with the engines of my external will.

With little time for pure thinking, I was spiritually dry and didn't consider eternity. Reflective thought and a deeper level of mindfulness were on the shelf. I was so concerned with inner space I didn't harken to look outward.

I love being old because now I can ponder on the wonder of Being. With age, my intimacy with the unseen becomes more acute. It is refreshing to transform and sustain my life from the inside out. In a spiritual revelation, poet Paul Claudet wrote "Lo! You are somebody all of a sudden."

I acknowledge that religions are the most humanistic disciplines of history, but I don't want to let dogma get in the way of the spirit. I have revised old prayers, nurtured by rote, with ones written in conversational form, beginning with "Hello". I find informality to be soothing.

Meditation has become refreshingly new, and with a spiritual breakthrough, I enjoy being alone with myself. The more in touch with my own feelings and experiences, the richer and more accurate are my guesses of what passes through another person's mind. It's a delight to awaken fresh thoughts.

Over my religious beliefs I cherish, I have superimposed a holistic concept of Being with the in-drawing touch of God. I accept that structured religion includes a rock foundation and an attempt to answer the questioning of the "how's" and "why's". Now I enjoy a new spirit of Totality with a simplistic and refreshing intimacy with Devine Existence. I sense being blessed by becoming aware of an infinite horizon.

To know the Creator, I realize I have to know creation. Four and a half billion years ago, God found space in the universe to form our solar system. He began with the sun, our fabulous star source of heat, light and gravity. Next, He made the planets Mercury and Venus, and then Earth in third place.

We will probably never find a scientific record of the earthly beginning of human life and mind. Geophysical experts confess they know little about these origins. But that doesn't stop me from crediting this event to Something Colossal, with whom I want to be close.

Geologist Robert Hazen reminds us that for more than 99.9 percent of Earth's existence, there were no humans. We are but an eye blink in our plant's history. I ponder our beginning of our planet and pity 47% of Americans who think God invented man 10,000 years ago.

Limiting awareness of and devotion to God to the birth of our Jewish/Christian religious beliefs 6,000 years ago, is short-changing Him. I find it exciting to sense an intimacy with the concept of eternity with a limitless horizon. It is like releasing God from a cage.

I appreciate what Pope Benedict XVI said three years ago.

It is beautiful to be elderly. It is necessary to discover in every age the presence and blessings of the Lord and the riches it contains. We receive the gift of a long life. It is also lovely to live at our age, despite some 'aches and pains' and some limitations. On our face there must always be the joy of feeling ourselves loved by God, never sadness. The wisdom of life, or which we are the bearers, is a great richness.

FINALE

T his sums up many ways I have made best the last stage of my life.

As a very joyful and appreciative fellow, I envy no one and feel sympathy for anyone who is not me.

It's fun to blend into today my yesterdays and tomorrows.

That's why I love being old.

> *The windowless window adrift into the sky,*
> *a golden-head parrot with red painted claws,*
> *a plant with feeling, whispering stones,*

a kid with tattoos and a ring in the nose,
a lonely stranger, no longer a stranger -
this is my world – a wonderful world.

Armiger Jagoe, TMBOOE

49205242R00067

Made in the USA
Columbia, SC
19 January 2019